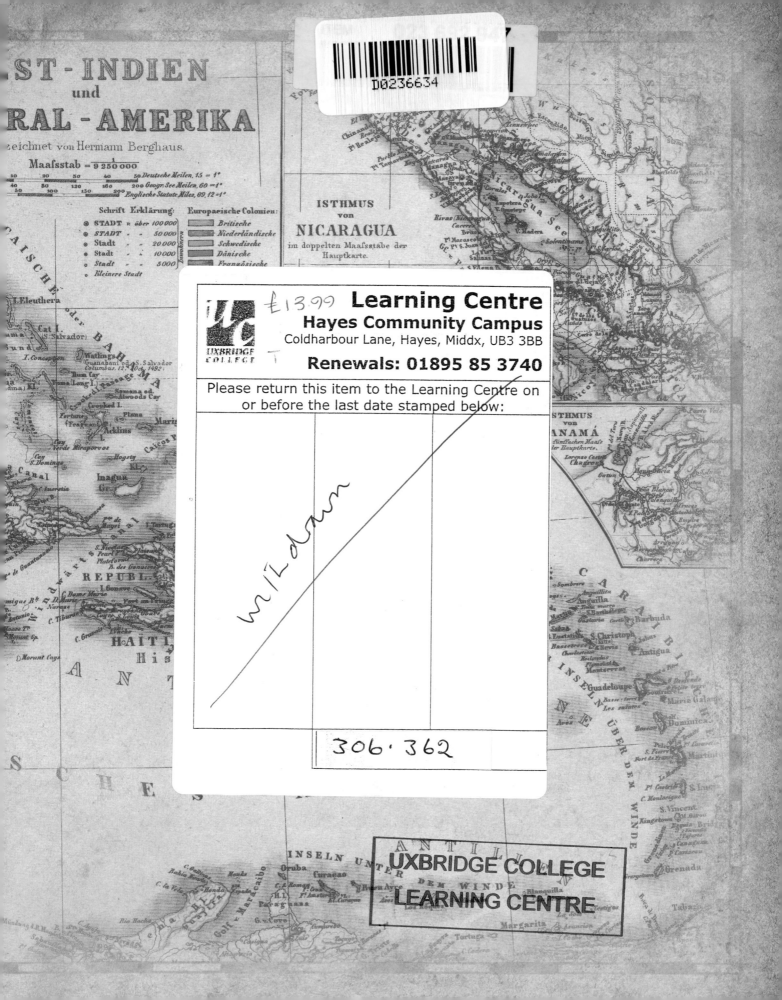

ST - INDIEN
und
RAL - AMERIKA

zeichnet von Hermann Berghaus.

Maaßstab = 1/9 250 000

Schrift Erklärung:
Europaeische Colonien:
- STADT u. über 100 000 — Britische
- STADT - 50 000 — Niederländische
- Stadt - 20 000 — Schwedische
- Stadt - 10 000 — Dänische
- Stadt - 5000 — Französische
- Kleinere Stadt

ISTHMUS
von
NICARAGUA
im doppelten Maaßstabe der
Hauptkarte.

ISTHMUS
von
PANAMÁ

WEST-INDIEN
und
CENTRAL-AMERIKA

gezeichnet von Hermann Berghaus.

Maassstab = $\frac{1}{9\,250\,000}$

10	0	10	20	40	50 Deutsche Meilen, 15 = 1°
40	0	40	80	120	160	200 Geogr. See Meilen, 60 = 1°
40	0	50	100	150	200 Englische Statute Miles, 69,12 = 1°

Schrift Erklärung:

- ● STADT ⋅ über 100 000
- ● STADT ⋅ ⋅ 50 000
- ■ Stadt ⋅ ⋅ 20 000
- ◻ Stadt ⋅ ⋅ 10 000
- ○ Stadt ⋅ ⋅ 5000
- ∘ Kleinere Stadt

Europaeische Colonien:

- Britische
- Niederländische
- Schwedische
- Dänische
- Französische
- Spanische

ISTHMUS von NICARAGUA
im doppelten Maassstabe der Hauptkarte.

LUCAISCHE oder BAHAMA INSELN

Providence Canal

I. Eleuthera

N. Providence

Andros

Exuma   Cat I.   (S. Salvador)
Sund   I. Concepcion
Watlings
Guanahani od. S. Salvador
Columbus, 12. Oct. 1492.
Gr. Exuma   Rum Cay
(Ferdinandina) Kl.   Long I.
Samana od.
Atwoods Cay
Crooked I.
Piana
Fortuna
(Fraganes)   Acklins   Mariguana
Verde Miraporvos
Hogety   Caicos Passage
Cay S. Domingo   Caicos
Inagua   Grand Turk
Gr.   Turk I.

Mouchoir - carré Bank

Silver Bank

Navidad Bank

Florida Strasse   Golf - Strom

Santaren Can.

Nicolas Canal

Gr. Bahama Bank

Alter Bahama Canal

Kl. Cayman   Cayman Brac
Gr. Cayman

C. Cruz
Santiago de

Windwarts Canal

REPUBL.

JAMAICA

Pedro Bank

DOMINICA
S. Domingo

HAITI   S. DOMINGO
Hispaniola

PUERTO

ANTILLEN

A R A I B I S C H E S   M E E R

Serranilla

Rosalind B.

Margate Riff

Serrana Cays

Roncador

Alt-Providence

INSELN UNTER

Oruba   Curaçao   Buen Ayre

Golf - Mardcaibo

Rio Hacha

Mündung d. R. Magd.

Resistance and Abolition

Dan Lyndon

FRANKLIN WATTS
LONDON • SYDNEY

First published in 2010 by
Franklin Watts
338 Euston Road
London NW1 3BH

Franklin Watts Australia
Level 17/207 Kent Street
Sydney NSW 2000

Editor: Tracey Kelly
Series editor: Adrian Cole
Art director: Jonathan Hair
Design: Stephen Prosser
Picture research: Diana Morris

Dan Lyndon would like to thank the following people for their support in writing this book; The Black and Asian Studies Association (BASA), Marika Sherwood, Arthur Torrington, Joanna Cohen and Joanna Caroussis. Thanks also to the Lyndon, Robinson, Cohen and Childs families.

This series is dedicated to the memory of Kodjo Yenga.

Acknowledgements:
Anti-Slavery International: 35, 39b. Art Media/HIP/Topfoto: 23b. Bibliotheque Nationale Paris/Bridgeman Art Library: 21bl. Reproduced with the permission of Birmingham Libraries and Archives: 34b. Bridgeman Art Library: 25t. British Library/Topfoto: 28. Mary Evans PL: 10, 23t, 30, 37b. Faberfoto/Shutterstock: 6. Fitzwilliam Museum Cambridge/Bridgeman Art Library: 29b. Getty Images: 29t. The Granger Collection/Topfoto: front cover l, back cover r, 8bl, 8tr, 9, 13, 14t, 17, 19t, 19b, 22, 26, 32, 39c. Houses of Parliament archives: 25b. Roger Howard/PD: 18. Library of the Religious Society of Friends: 34t. LOC Washington/Bridgeman Art Library: 31tr. Nanny Maroon Hills Productions: 20. NARA: 15t. National Maritime Museum: 24. New Haven Historical Society: 14b. PC/Peter NewarkAmerican Pictures/Bridgeman Art Library: 16. Photos12/Alamy: 15b. Private Collection/Bridgeman Art Library: 11, 27t, 38. Roger-Viollet/Topfoto: 12. Royal Geographical Society/Bridgeman Art Library: 21tr. Shutterstock: front cover1, back cover r. Eileen Tweedy/Art Archive: 5, 37t. Whitworth Art Gallery Manchester: 27b. Wilberforce House Hull City Museums & Art Galleries/Bridgeman Art Library: 31bl, 33t, 33b, 36.

A CIP catalogue record for this book is available from the British Library.
Dewey number: 326.8

ISBN: 978 0 7496 9029 8

Printed in China

Franklin Watts is a division of Hachette Children's Books, an Hachette UK company.
www.hachette.co.uk

Contents

Introduction

Throughout the brutal history of the Transatlantic Slave Trade that took place between the 16th and 19th centuries, Africans resisted enslavement at different times and in many ways.

Ways of resistance

This resistance included African villagers who attacked European slave ships to rescue African men, women and children destined for the plantations of the Americas and the Caribbean. Brave individuals led uprisings or escaped from the plantations and joined the 'Underground Railroad' in search of freedom. But also, in desperation, some enslaved people felt that their only resistance was to end their lives instead of living as slaves.

▲ *Detail from* Underground Railroad, *by Charles T. Webber, shows people helping slaves to escape.*

▲ *This engraving shows the 1791 slave revolt in St Domingue (Haiti).*

Resistance through survival

However, in many ways the most powerful example of resistance came in a different form: survival. Slave owners attempted to strip away any identity or humanity of the enslaved men, women and children. This was achieved by taking away their names (slaves were often given their owner's name), by denying them their culture (African music,

▲ *An evening prayer meeting of former slaves in Virginia, USA, 1864.*

religion and languages were often banned) and treating them as chattel (property) with the constant threat of physical punishment or even death.

So, what's inside?

This book continues from *Black History: Africa and the Slave Trade*, covering a period spanning the 17th–19th centuries. It contains case studies, personal accounts and in depth studies of key events and figures. Just before you turn over, though, think about this poem by Colonel William Mallory (1826–1907), a former slave who escaped to Canada and claimed his freedom in 1859:

I've won my way to Canada,
That free and happy land;
No more in cruel slavery
Need William Mallory stand.
Fare-the-well, old master,
That's enough for me!
I'm here, in dear old Canada,
Where colored men are free.

I will not have the driver's lash
Raised high above my head;
I will not have a peck of corn
Dealt out to me for bread;
For God, in His great goodness,
Came down to Calvary
And bore the burdens of the Cross
To set His people free.
Fare-the-well, old master,
That's enough for me!
I'm here in dear old Canada,
Where colored men are free.

Resistance in Africa

Africans were often enslaved as a result of war – with prisoners being sold as slaves – or by kidnapping. Resistance against slavery ranged from the people struggling against their captors, to redesigning villages so they became harder to attack. Although there is still little research on this topic, there are sources that suggest that resistance existed right from the very beginning of the Transatlantic Slave Trade.

Queen Nzinga

One of the earliest examples of resistance took place in Angola, in south-west Africa. In 1624, Queen Nzinga, leader of the Mbundu tribe, started a series of wars with the Portuguese who had come to Angola to get slaves for their plantations in Brazil and the Caribbean. She agreed a treaty with the Portuguese, but they did not keep their side of the bargain. As a result, fighting broke out and lasted for nearly 30 years. Queen Nzinga declared that her land would be 'free', meaning that no slavery would exist there.

Protection against slavers

Although most historical records of resistance to the slave trade come from the coastal regions, there were examples of resistance further inland. Communities built defences around their villages to make them harder to attack. These included large walls and barricades. Deep ditches were also dug and filled with thorns and poisonous plants. Rivers were diverted to make them harder to sail along and some villages were even moved to forests, marshes, caves and mountainous areas, which made them less likely to be discovered.

◀ Men armed with guns raid a village to capture prisoners for the slave trade.

▲ *This engraving from 1804 shows part of a high defensive wall surrounding a village.*

Protection against kidnappers

One of the ways in which Africans resisted was by setting up warning systems to prevent kidnappings. Olaudah Equiano (who was himself kidnapped and sold into slavery) described the situation in his village in his autobiography *The Interesting Narrative* ...:

"One day, as I was watching at the top of a tree in our yard, I saw one of those people come into the yard ... to kidnap ... Immediately on this I gave the alarm of the rogue, and he was surrounded (and tied up with rope) so that he could not escape till some of the grown people came and secured him."

Fighting back

There are also many examples of Africans fighting against the European slave traders. In 1454, the Italian explorer Alvise Cadamosto was attacked by 150 African men while on the River Gambia in Africa. Over 300 years later, similar attacks were still taking place. Abdel Kader Kane, an Islamic leader from Senegal, explained what would happen to anyone who wanted to trade in enslaved Africans:

"I repeat that if your intention is to buy (Africans) you should stay home and not come to our country anymore. Because all those who come can be assured that they will lose their life."

Resistance on the slave ships

The most frequent examples of resistance occurred on board the slave ships, with over 400 recorded slave revolts. These included armed uprisings as well as attacks from the coast, where Africans used boats to attempt to rescue captured friends and family. Despite the fact that most uprisings were unsuccessful, it has been estimated that as a result over 1 million Africans may have been saved from being transported to the Americas.

Serious threat

The seriousness of the slave ship uprisings and other attacks led to slave ship owners taking out insurance against 'insurrection'. They also made sure that the ship's crew

▲ *Slave revolts on board ships were brutal and bloody.*

were heavily armed with guns and knives, and that the African men, in particular, were chained below decks. Women were

usually not chained which meant that they could also participate in the revolts, not least by spreading information amongst the captives. Resistance also took the form of committing suicide, with many Africans throwing themselves overboard to drown rather than face life as a slave.

The Little George

One of the most successful slave revolts took place in 1730 on board the slave ship *The Little George*, which was sailing from the west coast of Africa to America with 96 slaves on board. The uprising started at 4.30 in the morning, when some of the Africans escaped from their chains and killed the three crewmen who were on watch. The captain, George Scott, and the rest of the crew were then locked away in the cabins and the ship was sailed back to the coast of Sierra Leone. When they arrived, the Africans made a deal with the captain that his crew would be freed if the Africans were also allowed to leave too.

▲ *Enslaved men attack the ship's crew in a bid for freedom. Most attempts were unsuccessful.*

Slave ship *Unity*

The records of the slave ship *Unity*, which came from Liverpool, reveal that there were a number of attempts by enslaved Africans to resist:

6 June 1770
The slaves made an insurrection which was soon quelled with the loss of two women.

26 June 1770
The slaves this day proposed making an insurrection and a few of them got off their handcuffs but were detected in time.

27 June 1770
The slaves attempted to force up the gratings in the night with a design to murder the whites or drown themselves, but were prevented by the watch.

Probably the most famous uprising took place at sea on the slave ship *Amistad* (below). On 2 July 1839, 56 enslaved Africans on board began to take over the ship led by a man called Sengbe Pieh.

▲ *The slave ship* Amistad.

◄ *A portrait of Sengbe Pieh (also called Joseph Cinqué).*

The uprising

Using a rusty nail to open up the hatches covering their deck, the enslaved Africans grabbed hold of knives that were used for cutting sugar cane and attacked the crew. Some of the crew escaped in a rowing boat, but the ship's cook and the captain were killed. Having successfully taken over the ship, Pieh now ordered the sailors to return the ship to Africa. However, the navigator tricked the Africans and ended up sailing into harbour in New York. Here, the United States Navy took control of the ship and took the Africans into custody.

The trial

The transport of slaves from Africa to the Americas was now illegal, so a trial was held in Connecticut to decide what should happen to the Africans. Should they now belong to the US Navy, or the Cuban owners of the ship, or should the Africans be allowed to go free? The main argument from the Africans' supporters was that a treaty had been signed between Spain and Britain in 1817. It made the transport of slaves from Africa to America illegal. This meant that the Africans had been kidnapped and should now be set free. The judges finally agreed that the Africans on board the *Amistad* should be freed and returned to Africa. Twenty had died in the struggle to take over the ship, but the surviving 36 Africans sailed back home in 1842.

▶ *The decision of the Supreme Court US versus* Amistad, *9th March, 1841.*

Did you know?

The *Amistad* story has been made into a film, directed by Steven Spielberg, and a reconstruction of the ship was built in 2000. The Freedom Schooner *Amistad* has been sailing to ports around the world ever since, to ensure the story of the *Amistad* is remembered.

▶ *A still from Spielberg's 1997 film* Amistad.

Resistance on the plantations

The work that enslaved Africans had to do on the plantations was hard. An overseer watched constantly to make sure they kept up a high work rate, otherwise they could be whipped. Other punishments included working on treadmills, wearing iron masks or having limbs cut off. However, many Africans found ways to resist their enslavers.

Runaways

Some slaves decided to risk running away rather than stay on the plantations. Their chances of success were slim as it was difficult to find food and shelter. The slave owners sent out gangs of men with dogs to track the runaway down.

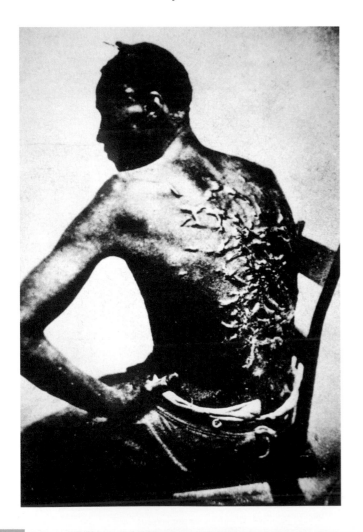

◄ Slaves, such as this man, faced the wrath of their owners every day. The back of this man is heavily scarred from repeated whippings.

Moses Grandy, who wrote a book about his experiences as a slave in America, *Life of Moses Grandy; Late a Slave* in 1843, described what happened when a slave ran away:

"They hide themselves during the day in the woods and swamps; at night they travel, crossing rivers by swimming, or by boats they may chance to meet with, and passing over hills and meadows which they do not know; in these dangerous journeys they are guided by the north-star, for they only know that the land of freedom is in the north."

Resisting on the plantation

Slaves could also resist their masters by working more slowly than they were meant to, or by playing 'dumb' – pretending not to understand instructions. Some slaves stole from plantations or broke farm machinery to reduce the profits of the owners. Herbs were sometimes made into poisons and given to the slave owner in his food. Another way for enslaved Africans to resist was to keep their old names, sing traditional African songs, play African drums and speak African languages together. The churches that they attended also blended traditional African ideas about religion with Christian ideas.

Underground Railroad
The Underground Railroad was a secret network of routes that many escaped slaves took from the south of the USA to get to Canada. Upper Canada had introduced the Slave Act in 1793 which saw the gradual abolition of slavery until the British Slavery Abolition Act 1833 made slavery illegal in parts of the British Empire. The Underground Railroad was made up of different safe houses, meeting points and transportation provided by 'conductors' who wanted to help the escaping slaves. The conductors came from many different backgrounds, including former slaves, white abolitionists and Native Americans. Harriet Tubman was a slave who escaped to freedom and spent many years rescuing over 70 slaves using the Underground Railroad.

◀ This engraving shows a runaway slave attempting to hide from the slave hunters.

Slave revolts

Revolts, or uprisings, were often the most violent ways for enslaved Africans to resist slavery. The prospect of slave uprisings terrified plantation owners, so any unrest was quickly stopped. But even unsuccessful revolts had a serious impact – they encouraged slaves to feel that their freedom could be achieved.

▲ *This statue in Barbados is of Bussa, and symbolises breaking the chains of slavery.*

Bussa's rebellion

On 14 April 1816, a large rebellion took place on Bayley's Plantation in Barbados. Led by a slave called Bussa, the rebels aimed to take over the island and replace the governor with their own leader, Washington Franklin. Bussa led 400 slaves into battle with the plantation owners, setting the sugar cane fields on fire. Soon the rebellion spread across the island. Eventually, soldiers from the West India Regiment were bought in to crush the uprising and Bussa was killed. Although Bussa's rebellion did not succeed, it gave hope to slaves on Barbados that they would one day be free. However the reprisals were severe; 144 slaves were executed and 123 sentenced to transportation. In total it has been estimated that 1,000 slaves were killed or executed as a result of Bussa's rebellion. A single white person was killed.

Nat Turner's rebellion

Nat Turner (1800–1831) was born into slavery and grew up in Virginia, USA, where he learned to read and write. Turner became very religious and preached the Bible. He believed he had a

HORRID MASSACRE IN VIRGINIA

The Scenes which the above Plate is designed to represent, are—Fig. 1. a Mother intreating for the lives of her children.—2. Mr. Travis, cruelly murdered by his own Slaves.—3. Mr. Barrow, who bravely defended himself until his wife escaped.—4. A comp. of mounted Dragoons in pursuit of the Blacks?

▲ *This American engraving shows the slave rebellion led by Nat Turner in 1831.*

mission from God to lead a revolt to free the slaves in Virginia, so he and seven close friends planned an uprising in 1831. They moved from house to house on the plantations, freeing the enslaved Africans and killing the white slave owners. In total, 55 white people were killed during the uprising, which lasted for two days before soldiers crushed it. Nat Turner escaped and hid for two months before being captured and executed. After the Turner rebellion, slave owners were always afraid that they could be overthrown – and enslaved Africans had a martyr and a hero.

▲ *In this engraving, Nat Turner (in the blue top) talks with fellow slaves in an 'imagined' scene.*

Slaves in Jamaica who had escaped and claimed their freedom were called Cimarrons (the Spanish word for 'wild') or Maroons. In the mid-16th century, the British fought against the Spanish for control of the Caribbean and made a deal with the Maroons to fight with them.

$500

JC4370

Queen Nanny

After the Maroons helped Sir Francis Drake fight the Spanish, Drake was presented with a medallion from Queen Elizabeth to commemorate his alliance with the Maroons. However, the good relationship between the British and the Maroons was short-lived. When the British captured Jamaica in 1655, there were a number of slave revolts led by

▲ *An image of Nanny of the Maroons appears on the Jamaican $500 note.*

the Maroons. There are few accurate sources that provide evidence about one of the most famous leaders of the Maroons, a woman known as Nanny. Although there is little doubt she existed, it is not known how much she took part in the fight against the British. It is believed that Nanny was an Asante (from Ghana) and lived in a Maroon community in the Blue Mountains (known as 'Nanny Town') where she raised crops. The Maroons began to raid the local towns, stealing food, setting fire to the sugar cane and liberating slaves from the plantations.

The Maroon Wars

The British got so fed up with the attacks by the Maroons that they sent in the army to stop them. The first Maroon war started in 1729 and lasted for over 10 years. 'Nanny Town' was well-protected as it was high up in the mountains with only a single path leading to it. This meant that the Maroons could see the British coming and could use guerrilla tactics to defeat them. In one story, Nanny helped to camouflage her men with branches and twigs, and made them stand still so that the British couldn't see them and would be surprised by the attack.

▲ *This photograph from c. 1908 shows people in the Maroon community.*

Legends of Nanny

Many legends are connected with Nanny, some of which are more believable than others. One story tells how Nanny was so powerful, she could catch bullets in her hands. Another story came from the time when the Maroons were close to starvation. Nanny heard voices from her ancestors telling her not to give up and the following morning she found some pumpkin seeds in her pocket. The seeds were planted and within weeks there were enough pumpkins for the Maroons to eat. Today one of the hills near Nanny Town is called 'Pumpkin Hill'.

Even after Nanny's death, in around 1733, the Maroons were strong enough to keep fighting against the British. They were eventually granted their independence in 1739 with their own lands in the east of Jamaica.

▲ *This engraving from 1759 shows the type of sudden attack launched by the Maroons.*

Toussaint L'Ouverture's rebellion

IN DEPTH

The most successful rebellion against slavery in the Caribbean came on the island of St-Domingue, led by Pierre Dominique Toussaint L'Ouverture. The rebellion raged between 1791 and 1804 and ended with complete independence for St-Domingue after the defeat of armies from France, Spain and Britain.

French education

Toussaint Bréda was born into slavery on the French colony of St-Domingue. He was fortunate to have an owner who taught him to read and write, and eventually granted him freedom when he was 33.

Toussaint was an intelligent man who read widely about new ideas of freedom and equality emerging from the French Revolution in 1789. He believed that enslaved Africans should have the same rights as people in France.

The military leader

Toussaint fought against the French in St-Domingue in 1791, after the French Revolutionary government (which had overthrown the royal family) had gone back on its promises to abolish slavery. He became an important military leader, and changed his name to L'Ouverture (which means 'the one who finds an opening'). In command of 4,000 troops, he showed great skill in military tactics and planning.

◄ Toussaint L'Ouverture on horseback after he became a general.

▲ *Toussaint L'Ouverture and his men are defeated by the French at Ravine aux Couleuvres.*

In 1794, the French government abolished slavery in the French Caribbean. As a result, Toussaint joined the French army and in just one week his troops won seven battles against the British and the Spanish. By 1797, Toussaint was the effective leader of St-Domingue. He signed a trading treaty with Britain and the USA, and freed the slaves on the Spanish island of Santo Domingo (Dominican Republic).

Toussaint and Napoleon

When Napoleon came to power in France in 1799, he was pressurised by plantation owners to reintroduce slavery. In 1802, a French army landed in St-Domingue, captured Toussaint and took him to France. He was put in prison in Paris, before being moved to a mountain fortress, where the conditions were so bad that Toussaint died of pneumonia in April, 1803. While on board the ship sailing to France, Toussaint said:

"In overthrowing me you have cut down in St-Domingue only the trunk of the tree of liberty, it will spring up again from the roots, for they are many and they are deep."

Toussaint was proved correct. In 1804 the French left the island – renamed Haiti. Haiti became the first independent black republic outside of Africa.

◄ *The death of Toussaint L'Ouverture in France, 1803.*

The resistance shown by Africans to their enslavement reinforced the belief among many campaigners in Britain that slavery was wrong and should be abolished. The abolitionist movement that developed in the late 18th century was led by people such as Olaudah Equiano, Granville Sharp, Thomas Clarkson, Elizabeth Heyrick and William Wilberforce.

▲ *This pro-slavery illustration presents the perceived happiness of enslaved people alongside the unhappiness of a poverty-stricken family in 1830s England.*

New voices

The abolition movement was the first time that a mass movement of people from different backgrounds and from all over the British Isles came together to campaign for a single cause. The important contribution from women to the abolitionist cause should also be recognised, as it represented the first time that women had participated in public on such a large scale.

It is also important to acknowledge the contribution that Africans made to their own liberation, such as Equiano, Ottobah Cugoano and Mary Prince.

▲ This chart was used to support changes to the enslavement of Africans. It was argued that the slave trade prevented land in Africa from being used to grow valuable crops, such as sugar cane.

Leading African

Leading African abolitionist, Olaudah Equiano, funded the publication and distribution of his autobiography. His supporters included Members of Parliament (MPs) and the Prince of Wales. Equiano considered himself an English gentleman; he married an English lady and had two daughters. This English identity also made his arguments against slavery in the British Empire even stronger.

Act of 1807

The 1807 Act abolishing the slave trade did not bring practical slavery to an end — in reality it did not even end slave trading. Enslaved Africans continued to work and be transported across the Atlantic, and conditions on the plantations did not improve. It was not until the Slavery Abolition Act of 1833 that slavery itself was abolished in some British territories (the Caribbean, Canada and Cape Town).

▲ A 1783 anti-slavery petition.

Campaign methods

The campaign methods of the abolitionists were very effective. Mass petitions gathered hundreds of thousands of signatures, while sugar boycotts (see page 33) cut the profits of the plantation owners. Tireless work was done by people such as Thomas Clarkson, who toured Britain revealing the horrors of the slave trade. This was matched by the pressure MPs such as William Wilberforce, and later Sir Thomas Buxton, brought to bear on Parliament.

Africans in Britain

While the vast majority of enslaved Africans were taken across the Atlantic, there were still African slaves in Britain from the middle of the 17th century until the abolition of slavery in 1833, and in some cases afterwards. The court cases bought by Africans, especially the Somerset Case, were critically important in changing the legal landscape at a time when the supporters of slavery were very powerful.

Katherine Auker

An early example of an African attempting to use the law to gain freedom happened in 1690. Katherine Auker, who had been brought to England on a trip from Barbados by her owner Robert Rich, had herself baptised. This meant that as a Christian, it should have been impossible for Rich to keep Auker as a slave. He threw her out onto the streets, but refused to give up ownership of her and prevented her from finding work elsewhere. Auker took the case to court and won the right to get paid work. However, her victory was temporary – she was taken back into slavery when Rich returned once more to Britain from Barbados to claim her.

◀ *It was not uncommon for plantation owners to have young female slaves in attendance.*

The Somerset Case

James Somerset was a slave who had run away from his owners when they brought him to Britain from Jamaica. He was recaptured and imprisoned on a ship due to return to Jamaica. However, friends rescued him and the case was bought to court. On 22 June 1792, Chief Justice Lord Mansfield delivered his judgement in the Somerset Case, which stopped any person (including slaves) being removed from England against their will. According to a report in a London newspaper, 200 black people gathered a few days later:

"…at a public house in Westminster, to celebrate the triumph which their brother Somerset had obtained over Mr Stewart, his master."

African-Britons campaign

One of the most overlooked aspects of the struggle to end the slave trade, and slavery itself, has been the contribution of Africans in Britain and the Americas to their own liberation. Leading African-Briton abolitionists, such as Olaudah Equiano and Ottabah Cugoano (1757–unknown), along with others, joined organisations such as the Sons of Africa to campaign against slavery. They wrote letters to newspapers, published books against the slave trade and supported the Parliamentary campaign around the country.

► *This is believed to be the only portrait of Ottabah Cugoano (right). He is shown serving fruit to Richard Cosway and his wife.*

▲ *An anti-slavery poster by Reverend Theodore Parker, 1851.*

27

Olaudah Equiano the abolitionist

Born in West Africa in 1745, Olaudah Equiano was captured and sold into slavery at the age of eleven. His first owner was a Royal Navy captain, who brought him to Greenwich, London, where he was taught to read and write by the Guerin sisters, the captain's relatives. Equiano eventually bought his freedom for £40 earned from small trading, and spent the rest of his life campaigning against the slave trade.

▲ *A portrait of Olaudah Equiano c.1789.*

The campaigner

Equiano had established himself as an important and effective campaigner against slavery even before he published his autobiography *The Interesting Narrative of Olaudah Equiano, or Gustavus Vassa, the African* in 1789.

He was a regular letter writer and in particular wrote many letters to newspapers around the country. Equiano argued passionately that slavery was wrong and that it was against the teachings of the Bible:

"Surely this traffic [of slaves] cannot be good, which spreads like a disease and damages every thing it touches … [which denies the] right[s] of mankind, equality and independency, and gives one man [power] over his fellows which God could never intend! For it raises the owner to a [position] as far above man as it depresses the slave below it."

Call for free trade

Equiano also argued that Britain could make more money from trading with Africa instead of enslaving her people:

▲ *Enslaved Africans in the hold of a slave trading ship.*

"I doubt not, if a system of [trade] was established (set up) in Africa, the demand for [British goods e.g. cloth, pots] would most rapidly increase, as the [Africans] will adopt the British fashions, manners, customs etc... A commercial [relationship] with Africa opens up an inexhaustible source of wealth to the manufacturing interests of Great Britain ... the manufacturers of this country ... will ... have [many jobs] by supplying the African markets."

▲ *New Hall tea set c.1800, just one example of goods being produced in Britain at the time.*

Equiano's book was the first to show the reality of the Transatlantic Slave Trade, including evidence of the Middle Passage, and the terrible conditions faced by slaves in the Caribbean and southern United States.

The book tour

Equiano was able to fund the publication and distribution of his autobiography by collecting subscriptions. By the time the 9th edition was published in 1794, over 1,000 people had subscribed to the book including the Prince of Wales and many MPs. This income also meant Equiano could travel to speak at meetings of the Society for the Abolition of the Slave Trade (see pages 30–31) and other abolitionist groups. Equiano died in 1797 aged 52, ten years before the slave trade was abolished. However, he made an enormous contribution to the abolitionist cause. Equiano's autobiography was translated into many different languages and has barely been out of print since its publication over 200 years ago.

Society for the Abolition of the Slave Trade

The first meeting of the Society for the Abolition of the Slave Trade took place on 22 May 1787, when 12 men met in a London printing shop to commit themselves to the abolitionist cause. From small beginnings emerged one of the most effective campaigning groups of the modern era.

Stopping the trade

The driving forces behind the Society were Granville Sharp and Thomas Clarkson, supported by William Wilberforce and the African abolitionist Olaudah Equiano. The initial campaign was against the slave trade rather than the practice of slavery.

▲ Granville Sharp (right) became known for his defence of Black rights.

The group felt this was a more realistic target that would have more success in Parliament, where many MPs had interests connected with the slave trade. The campaign to ban slavery itself and free enslaved Africans would come later.

Granville Sharp

Granville Sharp was born in Durham in 1735. He became known as a 'defender of the Negro' for his work supporting runaway slaves and on the case of the slave ship *Zong*, where 133 enslaved Africans had been thrown overboard. Sharp became knowledgeable in the law relating to slavery, and used this to great effect in the Somerset Case (see page 27). He was an original member of the Society for the Abolition of the Slave Trade. His works included 'A Representation of the Injustice and Dangerous Tendency of Tolerating Slavery', in 1769 – the first anti-slavery writing to be published in England. Sharp died in 1813, still campaigning for the end of slavery.

Thomas Clarkson

Another original member of the Society, Thomas Clarkson (1760–1846), collected evidence used to promote the anti-slavery cause. One of the most powerful tools Clarkson used was a set of drawings of the slave ship *Brookes*. These images (right) showed how enslaved Africans were transported in terrible conditions.

Clarkson travelled around Britain to spread the abolitionist message, even going to the slave-trading cities of Bristol and Liverpool at personal risk. Clarkson wrote pamphlets and letters in favour of abolition throughout his life. In 1807, he campaigned for the Abolition of the Slave Trade Act. He died in 1846 having seen the Abolition and Emancipation Acts passed by Parliament.

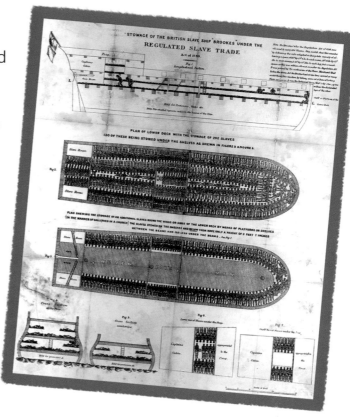

▲ *Diagrams showing the capacity of the British slave ship* Brookes.

▲ *Thomas Clarkson with samples of goods from Africa (right).*

Did you know?

Bristol and Liverpool were the main British ports involved in the Transatlantic Slave Trade. From 1697 to 1807, over 2,000 ships sailed from Bristol to the West Indies with slaves, and the profits from the trade brought the city great wealth. Slave trading was also a main factor in Liverpool's prosperity in the 18th century. Almost 1.5 million Africans were transported across the Atlantic on slave ships built or repaired in Liverpool.

Am I not a man and a brother?

The campaign against the slave trade and slavery kept its focus over many years, with dedicated people lending their time and talents. Along with famous contributors, vast numbers of people from all corners of Britain united to fight for a single cause. Abolitionists used many tactics to put pressure on Parliament to support abolition. These included petitions, boycotts and mass marketing techniques including creating their own badge and logo.

Signing petitions

The first petitions to end the slave trade were presented to Parliament in 1787 and by the end of that year over 100 had been collected with over 60,000 names on them. By 1792, this had increased to more than 500 petitions with an estimated 400,000 signatures. These petitions were signed by ordinary working people around the country who opposed the treatment of enslaved Africans. The petitions worked to increase the pressure on members of Parliament to support bills put forward to the House of Commons to abolish the slave trade.

▲ *Anti-slavery meetings were held to promote the rights of Black Africans.*

▲ *This Wedgwood medallion shows a slave with the words: 'Am I Not a Man and a Brother?'*

Branding logo

One of the most effective ways of spreading the abolitionist message, particularly to a population where most struggled to read and write, was to use images and slogans. The famous pottery businessman Josiah Wedgwood was a supporter of the campaign. He agreed to manufacture cameos (oval pieces of jewellery or pottery) featuring the image and slogan of the Society for the Abolition of the Slave Trade – an African man kneeling down in chains with the words 'Am I not a man and a brother?' underneath. A later version also appeared with the words 'Am I not a woman and a sister?' The images appeared on many different every day items including teacups, brooches, bracelets and even cufflinks.

Anti-sugar boycotts

When the first attempt to outlaw the slave trade failed in 1791, the abolitionists tried to find a different way to apply pressure. Now it used the economic power that abolitionists held. As so much money was made from the sugar industry, which survived almost entirely using the labour of enslaved Africans, a boycott of slave-grown sugar was launched. Within a year, over 400,000 people were boycotting sugar from the Caribbean and instead were buying sugar from India. It has been estimated that sales of sugar fell by nearly a half at the height of the boycott.

One of the most striking aspects of the sugar boycotts was the contribution made by women to the campaign, at a time when their participation in public life was limited.

▲ *A jug with an anti-slavery message produced as part of the anti-slavery campaign.*

The Abolition Acts

Towards the end of the 18th century, pressure was growing to bring the Transatlantic Slave Trade to an end. The activities of the abolitionists, including hundreds of petitions, letters and meetings combined with the anti-sugar boycotts, led to the parliamentary campaign to stop the trade in enslaved Africans. William Wilberforce (1759–1833) was the most famous MP to support abolition. He was responsible for introducing many bills in order to achieve this aim.

William Wilberforce

Born in Hull in 1759, William Wilberforce became the MP for Hull in 1780. He became friends with Thomas Clarkson and Granville Sharp, and was persuaded by

▲ A portrait of William Wilberforce.

their arguments that the slave trade should be abolished. The first abolition bill was introduced with a four-hour speech by Wilberforce in 1791 but was defeated. The powerful West India Lobby – the supporters of the plantation owners who were making huge profits from slavery – were not going to give up easily. Wilberforce continued to introduce abolition bills every year until slowly the MPs were won over.

Slave Trade Act 1807

The tide turned in the abolitionists' favour in 1806 with the election of a new Prime Minister, William Grenville, who was a keen supporter of abolition. When a vote was taken on the Slave Trade Abolition Bill in January 1807, it was first passed in the House of Lords by 100 votes to 34, and then passed in the House of Commons by 283 votes to 16. The bill received the Royal Assent on 25 March 1807. The British slave trade was abolished, and as a result, British ships and people had to stop trading in enslaved Africans.

▲ *A procession in England, 1808, after the ban on the Transatlantic Slave Trade.*

Abolition of Slavery Act 1833

Ironically, one of the consequences of the abolition of the slave trade was an increase in the profits made by plantation owners. This was because many slave traders had found profitable ways to break the new law. The conditions on the plantations did not improve and there was an increase in the number of rebellions. The idea that slavery would be abolished gradually was becoming less respected, and pressure increased for its immediate abolition, particularly from Elizabeth Heyrick and women's anti-slavery societies (see pages 36–37).

Wilberforce retired from the House of Commons in 1825 and the leadership of the parliamentary abolitionist movement passed to Sir Thomas Buxton. The 1832 Reform Act led to an increase in the number of abolitionist MPs and in the same year, a large-scale rebellion in Jamaica also convinced MPs that the time had come to end slavery. The Abolition of Slavery Act was passed in July 1833, which outlawed slavery in the Caribbean, Canada, Cape Town and Mauritius.

▲ *In this scene from the 1832 Jamaica rebellion, freed slaves attack the plantation house.*

Elizabeth Heyrick, a Quaker from Leicester, published a pamphlet in 1824 called 'Immediate not Gradual Abolition'. This was a radical and powerful argument that called for the end of slavery and the continuation of the sugar boycotts that "may save (England) the annual tax of **THREE MILLIONS** now paid in the direct support of slavery". Heyrick travelled around Leicester visiting grocers' shops to check whether they were selling 'slave-grown sugar'.

Women abolitionists

In 1825, Heyrick, along with many other women activists in the abolition movement, attended a meeting in Birmingham and challenged the leadership to explain why women had been excluded from any positions of authority in the Anti-Slavery Society (which had replaced the Society for the Abolition of the Slave Trade). William Wilberforce (see pages 34—35), in particular, felt that women were unsuited to involvement in the organisation "[F]or ladies to meet, to publish, to go from house to house stirring up petitions – these appear to me proceedings unsuited to the female character [as it is said in the Bible]."

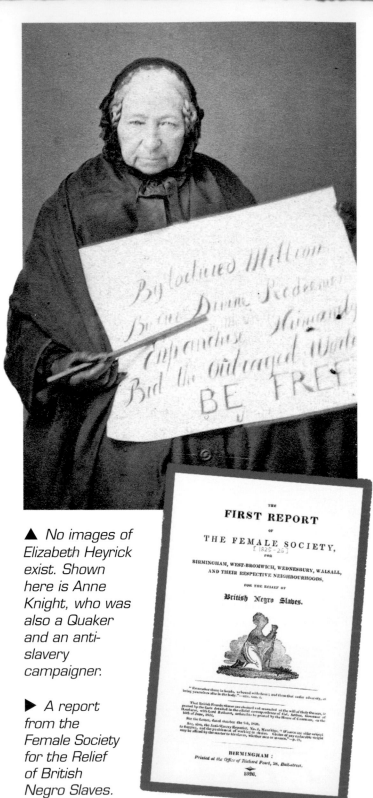

▲ No images of Elizabeth Heyrick exist. Shown here is Anne Knight, who was also a Quaker and an anti-slavery campaigner.

▶ A report from the Female Society for the Relief of British Negro Slaves.

THE
FIRST REPORT
OF
THE FEMALE SOCIETY,
[1825—26]
FOR
BIRMINGHAM, WEST-BROMWICH, WEDNESBURY, WALSALL,
AND THEIR RESPECTIVE NEIGHBOURHOODS,
FOR THE RELIEF OF
British Negro Slaves.

BIRMINGHAM:
Printed at the Office of Richard Peart, 28, Bull-street.
1826.

Wilberforce even went as far as trying to suppress Heyrick's pamphlet. As a consequence, Heyrick and others established the Birmingham Ladies Society for the Relief of Negro Slaves, and soon there were over 70 women's anti-slavery societies around the country.

Immediate action

Heyrick argued passionately that slavery should be abolished immediately and claimed that Wilberforce and Thomas Clarkson were taking far too long to achieve that goal. She even went as far as saying that, "the abolitionists have shown a great deal too much politeness and accommodation towards (the plantation owners)...Why petition Parliament at all, to do that for us, which... we can do more speedily and effectually for ourselves?"

Financial pressure

In 1830, a resolution was put forward at the meeting of the Anti-Slavery Society calling for immediate abolition. In order to make this demand more effective, Heyrick also suggested that the women's anti-slavery societies should withdraw their funds (around 20% of all donations) from the Anti-Slavery Society if it wasn't met. Her pressure was effective and the Anti-Slavery Society now started to push for immediate abolition. Within three years, slavery had been abolished in parts of the British Empire. Sadly, Elizabeth Heyrick did not live long enough to see the fruits of her dedication. She died in 1831 at the age of 61.

▲ A banner for the Anti-Slavery Society hanging in a street in Hull, England.

The legacy of the slave trade

The supporters of the 1807 Act believed that the consequence of the abolition of the slave trade would be an end to slavery. However, it soon became apparent that this was not happening. There were many loopholes in the Act, which meant that trading in slaves continued and profits from slave-produced goods were actually increasing.

Abolition effectiveness

Historians have estimated that over 2.5 million Africans were transported across the Atlantic (mainly to Brazil and Cuba) between 1811 and 1870. This was in spite of the British government trying to persuade other countries including France, the Netherlands and Spain to stop trading slaves. The Royal Navy's West Africa

▲ *A Royal Navy launch chases a slaving ship off the east coast of Africa c. 1876.*

Squadron also worked to capture ships still carrying slaves.

The 1833 Act brought an end to slavery in the Caribbean, Canada and Cape Town, although not immediately, and not in the rest of the British Empire.

Beyond Britain

Although slavery had been banned in many US states (called 'free states') as early as 1787, slavery continued to exist in the southern United States until 1865 when the American Civil War finally ended the practice. In Cuba, slavery continued until 1882 and in Brazil until 1888. The British still kept between 5 and 10 million slaves in India until slavery was abolished in 1843. The final act of abolition in the British Empire was not until 1936 in Nigeria.

▲ These troops, from the 4th US Colored Infantry, fought during the American Civil War.

Did you know?

A significant aspect of the 1833 Act was that £20 million was provided by the government to the slave owners as compensation for their loss of earnings. To this day, not a single penny has been paid to the enslaved Africans or their families for their suffering.

Slavery today

It would also be wrong to think that slavery does not exist today. There are slaves all around the world ranging from child workers in Asia to an estimated 800,000 men and women in Niger in West Africa. Even in Haiti, the home of Toussaint L'Ouverture and the first Caribbean country to abolish slavery, an estimated 200,000 children are being used as domestic slaves according to a recent report by the BBC. Organisations such as Anti-slavery are still fighting the same cause that Olaudah Equiano, Thomas Clarkson, Granville Sharp, William Wilberforce, Elizabeth Heyrick and thousands of others fought over two centuries ago.

▼ An enslaved girl in modern-day Niger, Africa. Her bracelets identify her as a slave.

Timeline – Resistance and Abolition

1441 The first record of Africans being enslaved and taken to Portugal

1562 Sir John Hawkins becomes the first Englishman to trade in African slaves

1624 Queen Nzinga challenges Portuguese slave traders in Angola

1729 The first Maroon wars in Jamaica

1730 Slave revolt on *The Little George*

1739 The Maroons are given their own lands in the east of Jamaica

1745 Olaudah Equiano born in Essaka in the kingdom of Benin (now Ghana)

1750–1800 The height of the Transatlantic Slave Trade – at least 3 million Africans are transported to the Americas

1770 Slave revolts on board the *Unity* from Liverpool

1772 The Somerset Case prevents enslaved Africans from being kidnapped in England and returned to the Caribbean

1776 The United States of America becomes independent of Great Britain

1787 Society for the Abolition of the Slave Trade founded

1789 Olaudah Equiano publishes his autobiography *The Interesting Narrative...*

1797 Toussaint L'Ouverture becomes leader of St-Domingue (later renamed Haiti)

1804 Haiti declares independence and abolishes slavery

1807 The abolition of the slave trade. West Africa Squadron of the Royal Navy formed to stop slave ships leaving Africa

1816 Bussa's rebellion

1817–18 France and Holland abolish slave trading. Spain and Portugal sign treaties with Britain to stop slave trading.

1831 Nat Turner's rebellion

1833 The abolition of slavery in the British Empire

1839 The *Amistad* Uprising

1865 Abolition of slavery in the United States of America with the 13th amendment to the Constitution

1936 Britain abolishes slavery in northern Nigeria

Key

- Resistance
- Abolition

Websites and Bibliography

Websites

http://www.blackhistory4schools.co.uk /slavetrade/ An excellent set of resources related to the Transatlantic Slave Trade, resistance and abolition.

http://books.google.co.uk/books?id=g_ kuS42BxlYC&printsec=frontcover The encyclopedia of Slave Resistance and Rebellion.

http://www.brycchancarey.com/ Brycchan Carey's excellent website about slavery, emancipation and abolition.

http://docsouth.unc.edu/neh/equiano1/ equiano1.xml Olaudah Equiano's autobiography *An Interesting Narrative*....

http://www.spartacus.schoolnet.co.uk/ USAslavery.htm A comprehensive guide to all aspects of the slave trade.

http://www.bbc.co.uk/history/british/ abolition/ Comprehensive guide to the abolition of the slave trade.

http://www.nmm.ac.uk/freedom/ Information and resources about slavery, resistance and abolition.

http://drb.lifestreamcenter.net/Lessons /Amistad/ Webquest about the *Amistad*.

http://www.nationalarchives.gov.uk/edu cation/lessons/lesson52.htm Online lesson about Bussa's rebellion.

http://www.citizenshipfoundation.org.uk /main/resource.php?s324 One of the best teaching resources about slavery and abolition.

Bibliography

Equiano O, *The Interesting Narrative of Olaudah Equiano or Gustavus Vassa the African*, Penguin, 1996

Foster N, *Out of Slavery*, Redcliffe Publishing, 2004

Fryer P, *Staying Power, the History of Black People in Britain*, Pluto Press, 1984

Hinds D, *Black Peoples of the Americas*, Collins Educational, 1992

Hosking T, *Black People in Britain 1650–1850*, Macmillan, 1984

Lester J, *To be a Slave*, Puffin Books, 1998

Rees B and Sherwood M, *Black Peoples of the Americas*, Heinemann, 1992

Rees R, *Britain and the Slave Trade*, Heinemann, 1995

Sherwood K and Sherwood M, *Britain, the slave trade and slavery from 1562 to the 1880s*, Savannah Press, 2007

Sherwood M, After Abolition, *Britain and the Slave Trade since 1807*, I B Tauris & Co, 2007

Smith N, *Black Peoples of the Americas*, OUP, 1992

Torrington A et al (Ed), *Equiano, Enslavement, Resistance and Abolition*, Equiano Society and Birmingham Museums and Art Gallery, 2007

Walvin J, *Slavery to Freedom*, Pitkin Publishing, 2007

Glossary

Abolition
To put an end to something completely.

Abolitionist
Someone who wanted to abolish the slavery of Black Africans.

Alliance
A formal friendship made between countries or peoples.

Americas
The word used to describe all the lands of both North and South America.

Barricade
A temporary defensive barrier.

Boycott
Refuse to have anything to do with a product or a country.

Calvary
The hill outside Jerusalem where Jesus Christ was crucified.

Christianity
The religion based on the teachings of Jesus Christ.

Culture
The arts, beliefs and traditions of a particular society.

Emancipation
To be set free.

Grating
A criss-cross of metal or wood placed over an opening to let air circulate or to prevent escape.

Guerrilla
A type of fighting carried out by people who do not belong to a normal army. Guerrilla forces tend to use surprise attacks and sabotage – planned destruction of supplies and materials – to fight the enemy.

Hatch
A movable covering over an opening or door, especially in the deck of a ship.

Insurrection
A word for an uprising or rebellion.

Maroons
From the Spanish word *cimarron*, meaning 'wild' or 'untamed'. The Maroons were escaped slaves living in Jamaica's mountain areas.

Middle Passage
The part of the Transatlantic Slave Trade, where enslaved Africans were taken from Africa to the Americas. The journey lasted between 6 and 8 weeks and many Africans died from the terrible conditions.

Negroes
Word used to describe black people from Africa – now considered by many to be offensive.

Overseer
Large landowners used an overseer to make the slaves work as hard as possible on the plantations.

Plantation
Large farms that the enslaved Africans were forced to work on, growing crops such as sugar, tobacco and cotton.

Slavery
When someone is forced to work for another person and loses all of their freedom and rights.

Subscription
A sum of money paid for receiving a magazine, newspaper or membership of a club.

Sugar industry
The growing, harvesting, processing and selling of sugar, particularly sugar cane.

Transatlantic Slave Trade
The name given to the enslavement and forced removal of millions of Africans from Africa to the Americas between the 16th and 19th centuries.

Transportation
To send a criminal abroad to a foreign country as a punishment. Once they'd arrived they had to work for a set amount of time, or even for the rest of their lives, on government projects such as road building.

Treadmill
A machine that is made to rotate by the walking action of a person or animal.

Underground Railroad
The network of safe houses and people which helped slaves to escape from the southern USA to 'free' areas in North America.

Watch
The person who has to keep a look out for danger, especially at night.

West Indies
Large group of islands in the Caribbean Sea and including Barbados, Jamaica, Antigua and the Turks and Caicos Islands.

Index

These are the lists of contents for the titles in *Black History*:

2 7

HOW DO SCIENTISTS
EXPLORE SPACE?

Robert Snedden

www.raintreepublishers.co.uk
Visit our website to find out more information about Raintree books.

To order:
☎ Phone 0845 6044371
▤ Fax +44 (0) 1865 312263
▣ Email myorders@raintreepublishers.co.uk

Customers from outside the UK please telephone +44 1865 312262

Edited by Andrew Farrow, Adam Miller, and Adrian Vigliano
Designed by Marcus Bell
Original illustrations © Capstone Global Library Ltd (2011)
Illustrated by KJA-artists.com
Picture research by Hannah Taylor
Originated by Capstone Global Library Ltd
Printed in China by South China Printing Company Ltd

ISBN 978 1 406 22624 9 (hardback)
15 14 13 12 11
10 9 8 7 6 5 4 3 2 1

British Library Cataloguing in Publication Data
Snedden, Robert
How do scientists explore space?. – (Earth, space, and beyond)
A full catalogue record for this book is available from the British Library.

Acknowledgements
We would like to thank the following for permission to reproduce photographs: Corbis pp. 4 (©Reuters/ HO), 16 (©REUTERS/NASA-Johns Hopkins University Applied Physics Laboratory/Carnegie Institution of Washington), 19 (©kyodo/XinHua/Xinhua Press), 20 (©Reuters), 28 (©Reuters TV), 31 (©NASA), 36 (©NASA/ STScI), 37 (©NASA/ STScI), 38 (©epa); Corbis SABA p. 9 (©Najlah Feanny); Getty Images p. 5 (amana images); ©Justin Knight p. 33; NASA pp. 8, 12 (JPL), 13 (JPL-Caltech), 14, 18 (JPL), 21 (JPL-Solar System Visualization Team), 22, 23, 29, 30, 32 (ESA/ G.Bacon), 34, 40 (PIRL/University of Arizona); Science Photo Library pp. 6, 7 (©European Space Agency/ DLR/ Fu Berlin [G.Neukum]), 10 left (©Gemini Observatory/NOAO/AURA/NSF), 10 right (©NASA), 24 (©European Space Agency), 25 (©European Space Agency), 26 (©NASA), 39 (©Walter Myers); SETI p. 41; Shutterstock p. 15 (© Christian Darkin).

Cover photograph of astronaut in space reproduced with permission of NASA.

We would like to thank Professor George W. Fraser for his invaluable help in the preparation of this book.

Every effort has been made to contact copyright holders of material reproduced in this book. Any omissions will be rectified in subsequent printings if notice is given to the publisher.

EARTH, SPACE, AND BEYOND

HOW DO SCIENTISTS EXPLORE SPACE?

Contents

Some words are shown in bold, **like this**. You can find out what they mean by looking in the glossary. You can also look out for them in the "Word Station" box at the bottom of each page.

Sky watchers

The earliest space explorers were the first people who looked up at the night sky and wondered about the things they saw. The beginnings of space exploration took place from the ground with no more sophisticated tools than sharp eyes and enquiring minds.

These immense columns of gas and dust are big enough to swallow our entire solar system many times.

Ancient astronomers imagined patterns connecting the stars in the sky. These patterns are called constellations.

Fixed stars

The first sky watchers would have noticed that most of the objects in the night sky always kept the same positions relative to each other. They rose and set in orderly patterns that always stayed the same. People of different countries, such as the Greeks, Chinese, and Indians, named these patterns of stars after gods and heroes. The night sky became a storybook of myths and legends.

Wandering stars

The sky watchers of long ago also saw that there were some objects that didn't follow regular paths. The ancient Greeks called them *planetes* (wanderers) from which we get our word "planet". The early observers built up precise records of the movements of stars and planets across the night sky. These observations became the basis of the modern science of **astronomy**, the study of everything that lies beyond Earth's **atmosphere**.

Aristarchus

Aristarchus, who lived over 2,200 years ago, was one of the greatest **astronomers** of ancient Greece. He used his observations to work out the sizes and distances of the Sun and Moon. He had no sophisticated instruments with which to make measurements and the answers he got were wrong, but his methods were correct. He correctly worked out that the Sun was very much bigger than Earth and he believed that Earth moved around the Sun. It would be almost 1,800 years before this idea was accepted.

Navigation

The patterns of stars are called **constellations**. First labelled in ancient times, modern astronomers still use constellations as a convenient way to divide and describe the night sky.
We can also use the stars to find out where we are on Earth. For example, for centuries people have known that facing Polaris, the North Star, means that they are facing north. Hundreds of years ago sailors had starcharts that told them how far above the horizon a star should be. Measuring the angle of the star above the horizon told them how far north or south they were.

Where are the Martians?

Even looking through a powerful telescope the planet Mars looks no bigger than a golf ball. It is hard to see much surface detail. Astronomers such as the Italian Giovanni Schiaparelli (1835–1910) and the American Percival Lowell (1855–1916) studied Mars through telescopes and saw channels, or *canali* in Italian, stretching out over the planet. Lowell was sure these were human-made canals, evidence that there was intelligent life on Mars. Other astronomers disagreed, but very soon the idea of walking, talking Martians became part of popular culture. Belief in Martians like these was finally put to rest when the space probe Mariner 4 reached Mars in 1965. It sent back pictures of an empty and barren landscape, covered in craters.

The telescope

Space exploration took a great leap forward with the invention of the telescope. As telescopes became more and more powerful, previously unseen wonders of the **Universe** opened up before the astounded eyes of astronomers.

The scientist Galileo Galilei (1564–1642) constructed one of the very first telescopes in 1609. Compared to modern telescopes it was not very powerful. After some experimenting, Galileo improved the magnification from 3 times to 20 times, which is similar to the power of telescopes used by birdwatchers today. However, using it Galileo discovered mountains on the Moon and spots on the Sun.

Percival Lowell drew this sketch of Mars. He was convinced that he saw canals crossing the planet's surface.

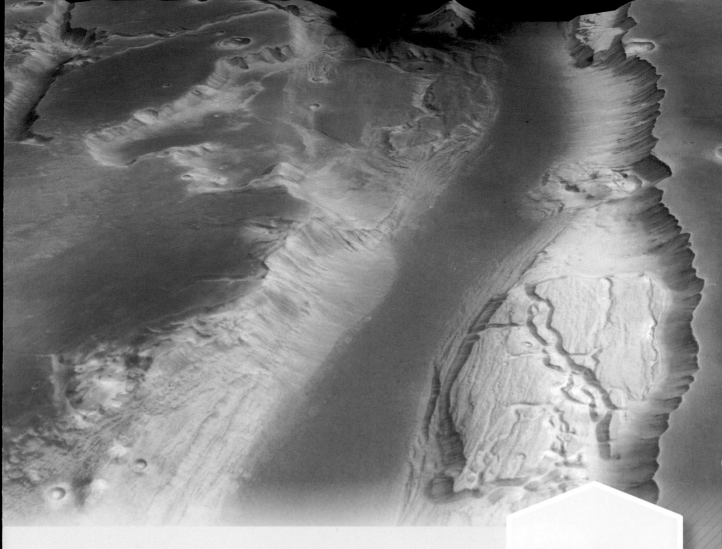

The Mars Express probe took this photograph of an ancient Martian riverbed. There has not been any water on Mars for billions of years.

Most amazing of all, Galileo discovered that the planet Jupiter had moons of its own. At that point it was widely believed that everything in the Universe rotated around Earth. The moons of Jupiter were proof that this was not the case.

Limits to seeing

Over the next three to four hundred years telescopes continued to get bigger and better, and astronomers continued to make new discoveries about the Universe. However, there is one important thing that limits what can be seen with a telescope – Earth's atmosphere. As light passes through the gases and dust in the atmosphere it gets distorted. This is why major telescopes are built on mountains. Because of pollution, the higher up you are, the clearer the air is.

Telescopes in space

In 1990, space scientists realized their dream of rising above the problems caused by the atmosphere. This was when the Hubble Space Telescope was put into **orbit** around Earth.

The Hubble Space Telescope in orbit, as seen by a visiting space shuttle crew.

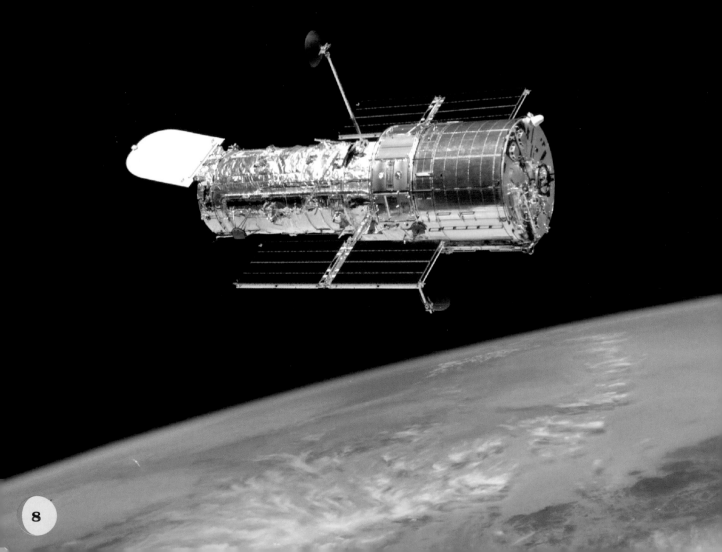

Hubble Space Telescope

The Hubble Space Telescope was carried into orbit aboard the space shuttle *Discovery* in April 1990. After another shuttle mission fixed the problems with its main mirror, Hubble began to send pictures back to Earth. The results were astounding, showing startling images of the furthest reaches of the Universe.

Dr Heidi Hammel of the Space Science Institute in Colorado, USA, is just one of many scientists who have made good use of Hubble's abilities. She used the telescope to see what happened to Jupiter in July 1994 when it was struck by a **comet**. "We discovered that it made a huge effect on the planet, from big black spots, to vast plumes of ejected material, to waves rippling through the atmosphere."

A number of shuttle missions have returned to Hubble over the years to replace parts that have failed and to keep its equipment up to date. Even so, Hubble's replacement, the James Webb Space Telescope is already being prepared for launch in 2014.

James Webb Space Telescope

More than 1,000 people in 17 countries are currently developing the James Webb Space Telescope. The telescope will have a giant mirror 6.6 metres (21.7 feet) across that will collect the faint light from the most distant objects in space (Hubble's main mirror is less than half that size). Getting a mirror this big into space is a challenge. The Webb team came up with a design using 18 hexagonal (six-sided) segments made of a material that is light, yet strong. The segments will be folded up to fit inside the rocket launcher. Once the telescope reaches orbit the mirror will unfold and observations can begin.

Dr Heidi Hammel has made excellent use of Hubble to study Jupiter. She will also be involved with the new James Webb Space Telescope.

Looking beyond light

We can see things in space because of the light that reaches our eyes from these distant objects. Stars produce their own light, and planets, moons, and other objects reflect light. When we see the Moon at night it is reflecting light from the Sun towards Earth.

However, visible light is not the only type of energy given off by objects in space. Light is just a part of the **electromagnetic spectrum**, a range of different types of energy that travel through space in the form of waves.

Radio astronomy

The longest electromagnetic waves are radio waves. Radio astronomers use radio telescopes to look deep into space. They explore giant **black holes** at the heart of **galaxies** and the dusty regions of space that light cannot pass through, where new stars are formed. It is possible to link up the signals from more than one radio telescope so that they act as if they were one huge telescope. This makes them incredibly powerful instruments for exploring the Universe.

Cold stars

The Spitzer Space Telescope (see page 11) discovered some of the coldest stars in the Universe. They are called brown dwarf stars and they are so cold and faint that ordinary light telescopes cannot see them. Some are as cool as 180°C (350°F), which is about the same temperature as a hot oven.

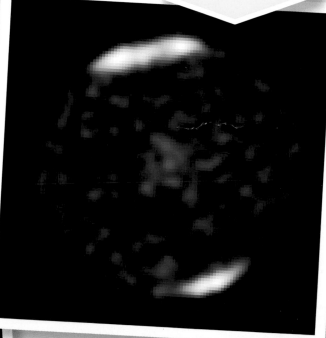

Two views of the planet Jupiter: on the left as it appears in infrared, and on the right as an X-ray image.

Infrared astronomy

We cannot see infrared waves, but we can feel them as heat. The warmth of the Sun comes from infrared radiation. Very little infrared radiation makes it through the atmosphere to reach the surface of Earth, but scientists are making new discoveries by using infrared telescopes in space, such as the Spitzer Space Telescope.

X-ray astronomy

At the furthest end of the electromagnetic spectrum are the high energy X-rays and gamma rays. The atmosphere absorbs nearly all of these high-energy waves from space, so X-ray astronomy wasn't possible until the invention of satellites. The X-ray universe turned out to look very different from the visible universe. Because X-rays are high energy it is mainly very hot objects in space, such as exploding stars, that are able to produce them.

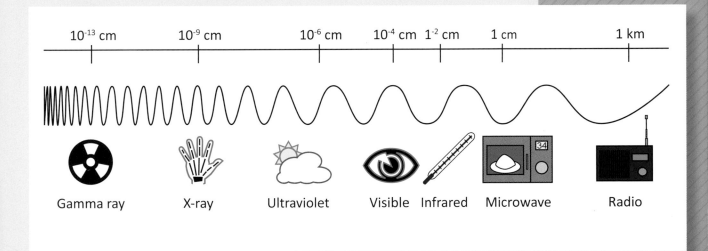

The electromagnetic spectrum is the name for a range of different types of energy that travel through space in the form of waves. Some of these waves, light waves, are visible to us but the others are not. All these forms of energy are given off by various objects in space. Using special instruments that can detect these waves, astronomers can build up a picture of the Universe that is richer than would be possible with our eyes alone.

WORD STATION
black hole region of space left by a star collapsing; gravity in a black hole is so strong not even light can escape it

11

Project planet

Planetary scientists investigate planets and their moons. They are interested in the processes that formed these objects and in the forces that continue to shape them today.

Up until the middle of the 20th century, all these investigations were carried out using powerful telescopes, both optical and radio. Everything changed when rockets that could send probes out into space became available.

The planet Mars as photographed by Mariner 4. This is one of the first images of another planet to be sent back from space.

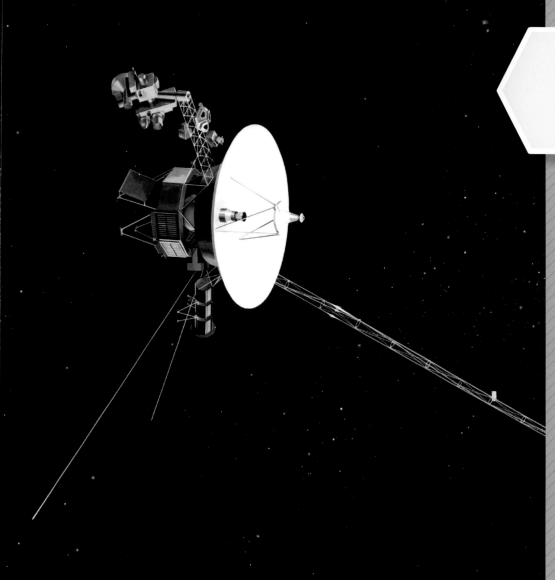

This image is an artist's impression of Voyager 1 as it travels through deep space.

Voyager's journey

One of the most successful probes is Voyager 1, which returned images of the giant planets Jupiter and Saturn and their moons in 1979 and 1980. Thirty years later, Voyager is the most distant probe from Earth and is still working. As it heads towards **interstellar space** it continues to send back information about the furthest reaches of the solar system. Voyager is so far away that it takes a signal from the spaceship almost 16 hours to reach Earth. Space scientists expect Voyager to keep operating until at least 2025.

First probes

The first **space probe** from Earth to reach another planet was Mariner 2, which flew within 35,000 kilometres (22,000 miles) of Venus in 1962. Since then a huge number of probes have gathered information on all of the major planets in the **solar system** and their moons.

Space probes changed the way we think about the other planets in space. Once they were little more than lights in the sky. Now they were places, whole new worlds, we had been to and begun to explore. Space probes have given planetary scientists the opportunity to see these distant worlds in a wealth of detail that could never have been possible from Earth.

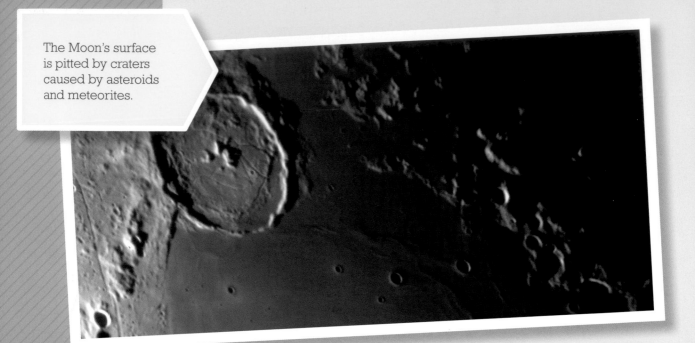

The Moon's surface is pitted by craters caused by asteroids and meteorites.

From Earth to the Moon

The closest object to us in space is the Moon. It is the brightest object in the night sky and the only one that is close enough for surface details to be seen clearly through a telescope. The Moon has a special position in the history of space exploration. It is the only other place in the Universe that people from Earth have visited.

Project Apollo

Project Apollo was the American space programme that first landed people on the Moon between 1969 and 1972. The Apollo missions discovered several things about the Moon that couldn't have been discovered from Earth.

Samples of rock were brought back to Earth. Examining these rocks told scientists that the Moon has always been lifeless. No trace of any life has ever been found in the Moon rocks.

Studying the rocks also showed that the youngest Moon rocks are nearly as old as the oldest Earth rocks. In its earliest history the whole surface of the Moon was an ocean of molten rock. These findings support the idea that the Moon was formed when another object collided with the young Earth, throwing huge amounts of debris into space. This debris gathered together to form the Moon.

Over millions of years, **asteroids** and **meteorites** pounded the Moon. The surface of the Moon is covered in a layer of dust and rubble left by those crashes. Because there is no air or water on the Moon, there is nothing to erode the rocks or wash the dust away.

The first space bases on the Moon will be small, with just a few buildings to support scientific study and exploration.

Robots to the Moon

India, China, and Japan have all successfully sent probes to the Moon in recent years. Japan is currently developing plans for a Moon base that will be operated by robots.

The first of the 300-kilogram (661-pound) robots is scheduled to arrive on the Moon by 2015. They will roam around the lunar surface on caterpillar treads. Their equipment will include **solar panels**, from which they will get their power, high-definition cameras, and a variety of scientific instruments. The robots will collect samples to be sent back to Earth by rocket. The next stage of the plan is for the robots to build a solar-powered Moon base near the south pole of the Moon by 2020. At that point astronauts might join the robots. Japan's scientists believe that a Moon base will be an essential jumping-off point from which to explore the solar system.

Messenger to Mercury

Mercury is the closest planet to the Sun. The glare from the Sun makes it very difficult to observe Mercury. So far, only two spacecraft from Earth have visited Mercury, the smallest planet in the solar system. Until space scientists saw the pictures they sent back they had little idea what the surface of Mercury looked like.

Slingshot through space

The first craft to reach Mercury was Mariner 10, launched in 1973. It was also the first spacecraft to make use of something called a **gravity assist**, or slingshot. Scientists have discovered that if a probe passes by a planet at just the right angle, the planet's **gravity** can be used to change its speed and direction. Mariner 10 used Venus to slow down on its way to Mercury, saving rocket fuel.

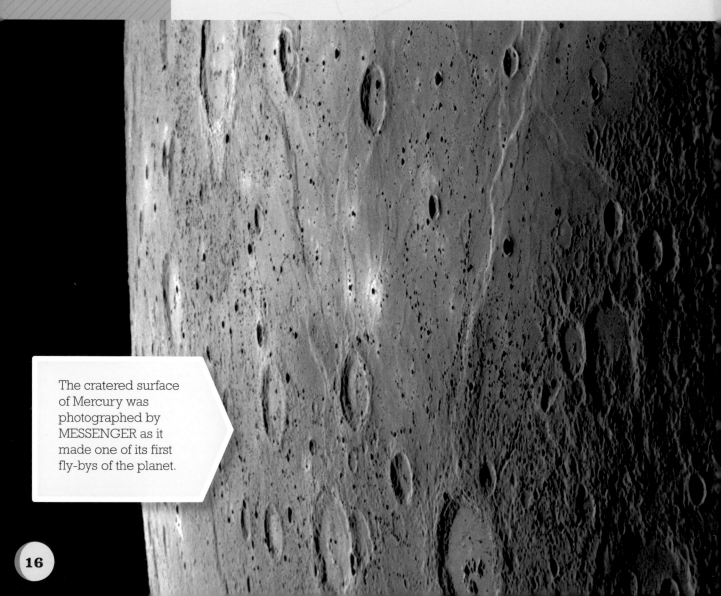

The cratered surface of Mercury was photographed by MESSENGER as it made one of its first fly-bys of the planet.

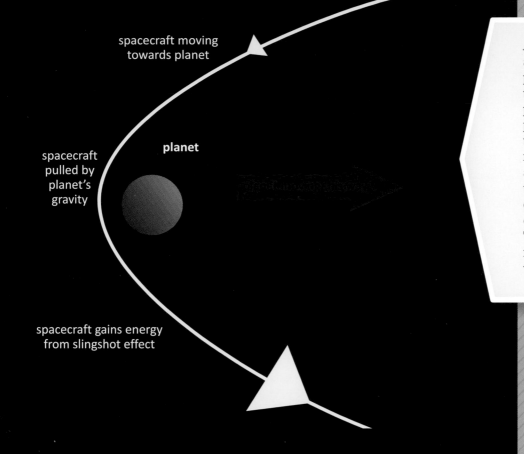

spacecraft moving
towards planet

planet

spacecraft
pulled by
planet's
gravity

spacecraft gains energy
from slingshot effect

A spacecraft approaching a planet is pulled towards the planet by the planet's gravity. If the approach is made at the right angle the craft can use the planet's gravity to change course and speed. This slingshot manoeuvre saves valuable rocket fuel.

MESSENGER

MESSENGER (the MErcury Surface, Space ENvironment, GEochemistry, and Ranging) spacecraft will be the first satellite to be placed in orbit around the planet Mercury. MESSENGER is on a complex looping, energy-saving flight path that sees it fly by Earth once, Venus twice, and Mercury three times before finally entering orbit around Mercury in March 2011. It takes a long time to reach Mercury by this route. However, it means that the spacecraft doesn't have to carry the large amounts of rocket fuel that would otherwise be needed to slow it down enough to enter orbit.

Louise Prockter is the lead instrument scientist for the Mercury Dual Imaging System (MDIS) carried aboard MESSENGER. The MDIS will help Prockter and the rest of the team investigate the different rock types on Mercury. She was one of the first to see the surface of an asteroid — now she's looking forward to a close-up view of Mercury.

"The pace of the mission can get quite hectic. The spacecraft keeps moving no matter what's going on in your life, and balancing all that can be a challenge."

Louise Prockter

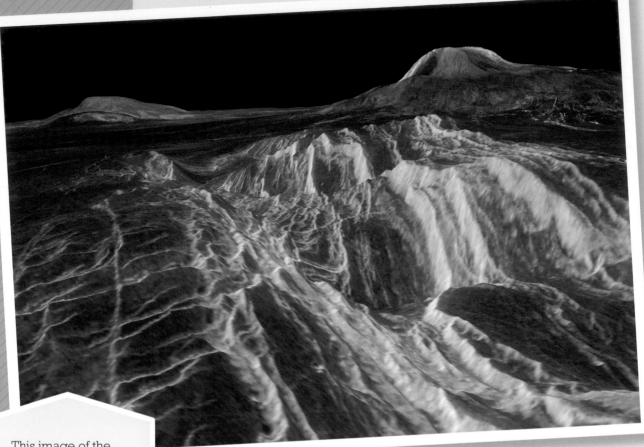

This image of the surface of Venus was created using radar images taken from the Magellan space probe.

Venus weather watch

We are used to seeing satellite reports of the weather here on Earth. Now there is a mission to take a look at the weather on another planet.

Akatsuki

The Japanese space probe Akatsuki (originally called the Venus Climate Orbiter) was launched on 21 May 2010 and was scheduled to enter orbit around Venus in December 2010, but failed to do so. Scientists will try again to enter it into orbit, but they will have to wait six years while Akatsuki travels once around the Sun! If they are successful, Akatsuki will be one of the first weather satellites to orbit another planet.

Akatsuki will try to explain the ferocious storm winds that blow across the surface of the planet. These rage around Venus at speeds of over 360 kilometres per hour (220 miles per hour). Called super-rotation, the winds travel 60 times faster than the planet itself rotates. At the moment scientists don't know what might be causing this.

On board Akatsuki are infrared cameras that can peer through the thick atmosphere to the surface of the planet. It is hoped that they might reveal the cause of the high-speed winds. Project scientist Takeshi Imamura is open-minded about what may be discovered. "We may be pleasantly surprised by the emergence of a greater mystery than super-rotation," he said.

Satellite partnership

When Akatsuki reaches Venus it will join the European Space Agency's Venus Express, which is already in orbit studying the chemicals in the planet's atmosphere.

"Venus Express and Akatsuki are like sister satellites, and a very good co-operative relationship has been built as we have progressed in our missions," Imamura said. David Grinspoon, one of the Venus Express scientists, agrees. "Venus [is] a really dynamic planet that's very changeable. Having Akatsuki there should help capture more vital clues to understanding Venus' mysteries."

Global warming

Venus is similar in size to Earth, but conditions there are very different. A thick carbon dioxide atmosphere blankets its barren desert landscape. Venus is hotter than Mercury, even though it is further from the Sun. Many scientists are concerned that Earth's temperature is rising. Is Venus a warning for the future?

Carbon dioxide is a **greenhouse gas**. The heat it traps has boosted the surface temperature of Venus to a sweltering 480°C (900°F). By studying conditions on Venus scientists hope to understand how conditions here on Earth might be changed if the amount of carbon dioxide in our atmosphere increases.

A rocket carrying the Akatsuki space probe lifts off from Japan's Tanegashima Space Centre.

A day on Mars

A Martian day is called a **sol** and Mars mission scientists measure the time a probe has been on the surface in sols rather than days. One Martian sol is 35 minutes, 39 seconds longer than one day on Earth.

Red planet rovers

Scientists have sent a number of probes to land on the surfaces of other worlds. Landers have visited the Moon, Venus, Mars, Saturn's moon Titan, and even an asteroid. Two of the most successful of these surface explorers have been the Mars Exploration Rovers, called Spirit and Opportunity.

Martian mission

The Mars rovers arrived on Mars in January 2004. Their main mission is to sample as wide a range of rocks and soils on the surface as possible. Scientists have found evidence that water once flowed on Mars. This water might have made it possible for life to exist on Mars long ago.

This artwork shows one of the Mars Exploration Rovers emerging from its protective capsule after landing on the surface of Mars.

Sunset on Mars. The Sun appears smaller than it does on Earth because Mars is much further from the Sun than Earth is.

Setting a course

When the rovers first arrived they took panoramic (full view) pictures of their surroundings. This helped the scientists to pick out places that looked worth investigating. Deciding on a rover's route across the Martian surface takes careful planning. Once the scientists have decided on their targets, the engineering team has to determine whether or not the rover can get there safely.

It takes 20 minutes for a radio signal to travel across space from Earth to Mars, so it is impossible to steer the rover in "real time". At the start of each day a set of instructions is uploaded to the rover. These instructions tell the rover where to go and what experiments to carry out.

Avoiding hazards

The rover is equipped with hazard avoidance software. Every few seconds the rover stops and examines the surface in front of it using a pair of Hazcams (hazard cameras). If there is a possible hazard ahead the on-board computer will instruct the rover to change course to avoid it.

Rover update

The Mars rovers have kept going far longer than scientists expected. By summer 2010, Spirit had powered down and contact had been lost. Scientists hope to regain contact when its batteries recharge using its solar panels. Opportunity is still going strong and continues to send back information.

Juno to Jupiter

The planets are not unchanging objects in space. Early in 2010 one of the two main cloud belts that circle the giant planet Jupiter completely disappeared. The Southern Equatorial Belt (SEB) is more than twice as wide as the entire planet Earth. Yet every now and then it vanishes, only to mysteriously reappear in a dramatic outburst of storms that circle Jupiter.

Planetary scientists would love to know why this happens. Planetary scientist Glenn Orton thinks that the cloud belt might not have disappeared. It is possible that it is hidden beneath other clouds that have formed above it. Orton has suggested that changing wind patterns on Jupiter have caused high-altitude clouds to form and cover up the cloud belt. But no one can explain why the southern belt should vanish while the northern belt remains.

"We have a long list of questions."

Glenn Orton

These photographs clearly show that Jupiter's Southern Equatorial Belt of clouds has disappeared.

Jupiter

Before
4 August 2009

After
8 May 2009

The Juno space probe is shown here being fitted with a heavy shield to protect it from Jupiter's radiation.

Juno

NASA's Juno probe, due for launch in 2011, may provide some of the answers. The journey from Earth to Jupiter will take five years.

Juno's highly sensitive instruments will map Jupiter in several different ways. It will measure its powerful magnetic field and strong gravity. It will look at Jupiter's atmosphere to see how it varies from place to place across the planet. No one knows how deeply the features we see on Jupiter actually go. Juno will probe deep beneath the clouds to find out what is going on inside Jupiter's atmosphere. Perhaps here it will find reasons for the mysterious vanishing cloud belt.

First views

When it arrives, Juno will enter an orbit that will take it over the poles of the biggest planet in the solar system. It will have views of Jupiter that have never been seen before. Amongst Juno's complex scientific instruments there is a colour camera. This was included to give people their first view of Jupiter's poles.

Comet encounters

The Kuiper belt

In 1951, after studying the paths followed by many comets, astronomer Gerard Kuiper suggested that there must be a belt of perhaps hundreds of millions of comets out beyond the orbit of the planet Neptune. In 1992, astronomers detected a **Kuiper belt** object (KBO) for the first time. Today more than 1,300 KBOs have been identified.

Comets are icy remnants left over from the formation of the planets. Some travel on orbits that take them in towards the Sun, then back to the outer solar system. As the comet approaches the Sun, radiation heats it. This causes gas and dust to boil off, forming the comet's distinctive tail.

Rosetta

The European Space Agency's Rosetta probe will be the first to explore a comet at close range over a long period of time. It is currently on its way to meet with Comet 67P/Churyumov-Gerasimenko in 2014. Rosetta will receive gravity assists from both Earth and Mars to speed it on its long journey.

When it arrives, the spaceship will go into orbit around the comet. It will spend the next two years accompanying the comet as it heads towards the Sun. A small lander will also be placed on the surface of the comet. A number of scientific experiments carried on board the orbiter and lander will carry out the most detailed study of a comet ever attempted.

The Rosetta probe made use of Earth's gravity to speed it on its way to its meeting with a comet in 2014. Opposite page: an artist has imagined how the probe might look on the comet's surface.

Comet approach

The first approach to the comet takes place before Rosetta's cameras are activated. This means that everything depends on the observations of the comet's path made from Earth being absolutely accurate. As Rosetta closes in on the comet it will fire its braking rockets. Rosetta's thrusters will fire for several hours as it slows to match the comet's speed. Once the first images reach Earth, the team will be able to make last minute adjustments to Rosetta's flight path. Eventually, if all goes well, it will enter an orbit just 25 kilometres (16 miles) above the comet's surface.

"It is absolutely mind blowing when you think of what we are going to do."

Rosetta project manager, John Elwood

Ice dwarves of the Kuiper belt

Some Kuiper belt objects are very big. One of the largest is Pluto, once considered to be the ninth planet in the solar system. In 2005 scientists announced that they had discovered a KBO that was bigger than Pluto.

Venetia, the Student Dust Counter

One of the instruments carried on board New Horizons (see page 27) is the Student Dust Counter (SDC), designed and built by students at the University of Colorado in the United States. It will measure the sizes of dust particles in space throughout the spacecraft's journey. The SDC was named Venetia after Venetia Burney, who suggested the name for Pluto when she was eleven.

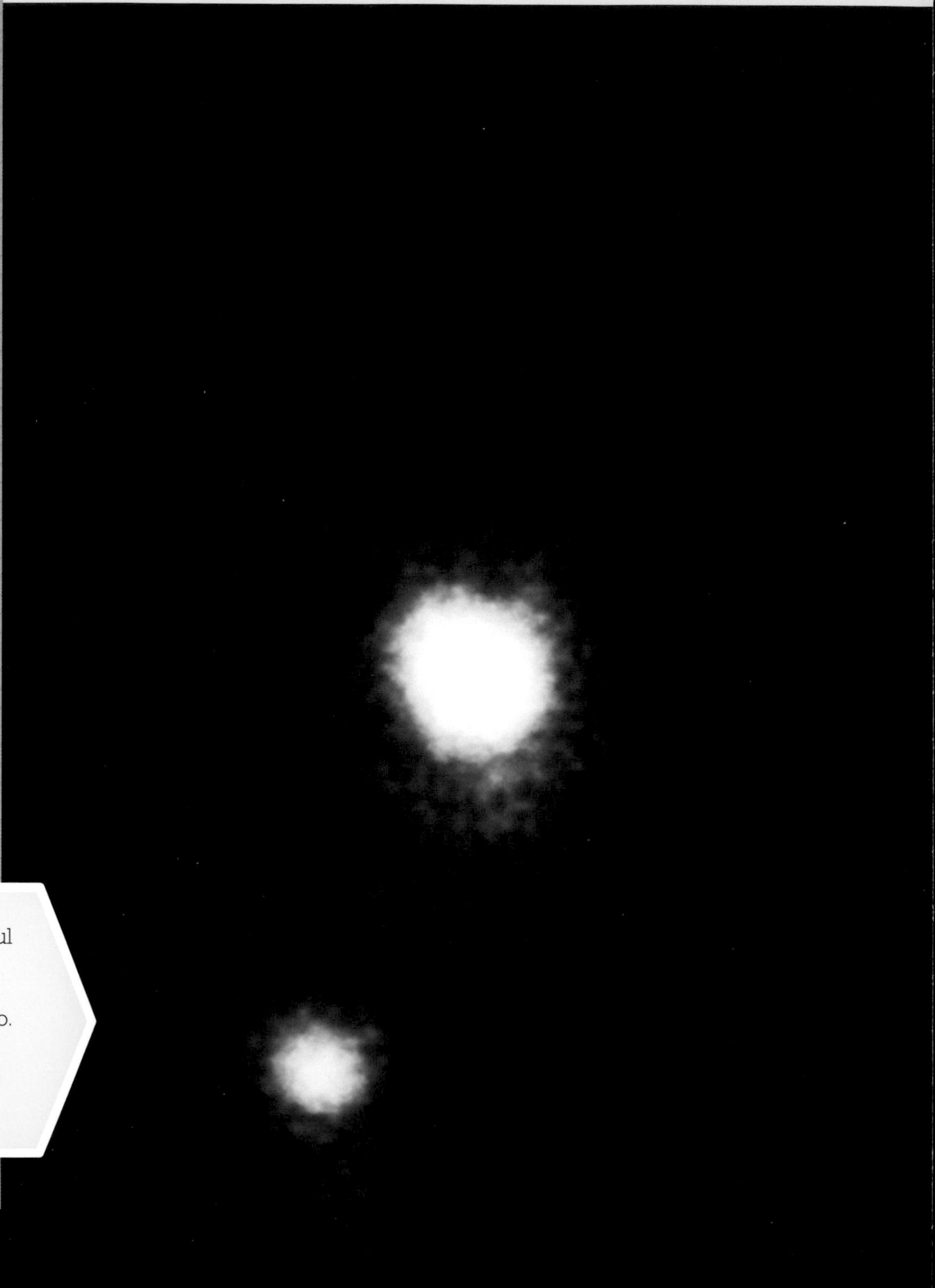

Not even the powerful Hubble telescope can capture a clear image of distant Pluto. The smaller object seen below is Pluto's moon, Charon.

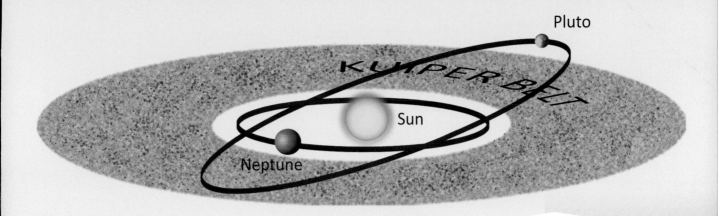

The icy objects in the Kuiper belt circle the solar system beyond the orbit of Neptune.

Dwarf planets

The discovery of Eris, as the new object was called, made scientists think again about what could actually be called a planet. They wondered if they should call Eris the tenth planet of the solar system. Instead of doing that they created a new class of dwarf planets. This would include Pluto, thereby changing its status as a planet. Today five dwarf planets are known: Ceres, Pluto, Haumea, Makemake, and Eris.

New Horizons

Launched at the beginning of 2006, the New Horizons space probe will encounter Pluto in 2015. This will be the first time this distant object will ever have been visited by a probe from Earth. For most of its long journey New Horizons is powered down into sleep mode to save energy, just as a computer monitor will go dark when it is not used for a while. Mission scientists will wake it up for 50 days each year to carry out instrument checks.

After its encounter with Pluto, New Horizons will continue on to investigate other KBOs. Investigator Alan Stern thinks it is important that we should send a spaceship to the Kuiper belt. He believes New Horizons will help us to gain a deeper understanding of the birth of the solar system.

"We're in the space exploration business and the outer solar system is a wild, woolly place. We haven't explored it very well."

Alan Stern

Solar explorers

Without a doubt the most important object in space as far as people are concerned is the Sun — the star in the middle of the solar system. More than 99 per cent of the material in the solar system is contained in the Sun and its powerful gravity holds everything else in place. There would be no life on Earth without its heat and light.

Genesis

Several missions have been launched to study the Sun. The Genesis probe was sent to capture material from the outer regions of the Sun's atmosphere and return it to Earth. These samples were collected using specially developed materials.

When the Genesis return capsule crashed back to Earth scientists were sure the mission would be a failure, but they still managed to find some usable samples.

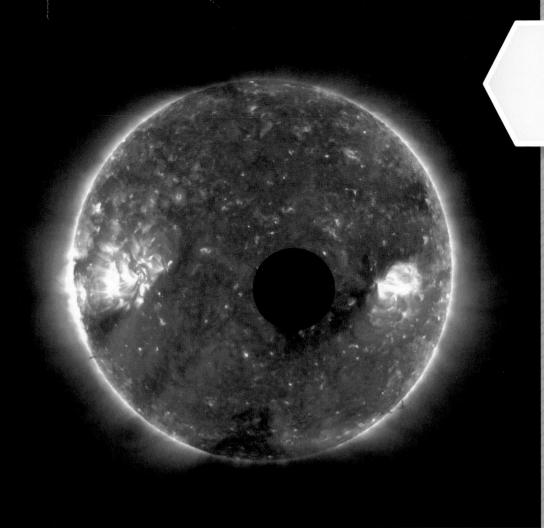

The STEREO B satellite captured this image of the Moon passing in front of the Sun.

Coronal mass

Every so often the Sun throws off material in an explosion called a coronal mass ejection (CME). Each one contains the energy of millions of nuclear weapons and travels through space at 1,600,000 km/h (1,000,000 mph). Chris Davis of the Rutherford Appleton Laboratory in England is using STEREO to study CMEs. "If one of these clouds reaches Earth, it has the potential to damage Earth-orbiting spacecraft, disrupt navigation systems, and cause power surges on the ground. We need to understand the extremes of this 'space weather' if mankind is to travel to the Moon and beyond."

At the end of the collection period Genesis closed up and a sample return capsule was sent back to Earth. Unfortunately, when the capsule returned to Earth, a design fault prevented its parachutes from opening. It crashed into the ground at high speed. Many of the collectors were shattered and scientists were concerned that the samples were contaminated. Luckily they determined that some samples were buried so deep in the collectors they could still be used for research.

Seeing in STEREO

The twin satellites of the STEREO (Solar Terrestrial Relations Observatory) mission are being used to capture never before seen images of the Sun. One satellite travels ahead of Earth in its orbit while the other follows on behind. You might think of them as being like left and right eyes, working together to build up a stereoscopic (3D) image.

SOHO

SOHO (the Solar and Heliospheric Observatory) is an international project operated jointly by the European Space Agency and NASA. Launched in 1995, it has been sending back huge amounts of data about the Sun to scientists on Earth. Using this information, researchers have been learning a great deal about our star and how it behaves.

SOHO being assembled before launch. The solar panels, seen flat against the sides at the bottom here, opened out once SOHO reached space.

CASE STUDY:

Saving SOHO

The SOHO mission almost came to a disastrous end in 1998 when a fault caused contact with the satellite to be lost. Scientists tried to make contact with SOHO using NASA's Deep Space Network (DSN) but there was no response.

What they thought was happening was that SOHO had gone into a spin with its solar panels nearly edge on to the Sun. This meant that it wasn't generating any power. The deep chill of outer space would freeze its batteries and fuel. The scientists calculated that there would be one point in SOHO's orbit where the solar panels would get most light.

Breaking the silence

After six weeks of silence, the DSN picked up the first signals from SOHO. This was the first sign that it could receive commands from the ground. Immediately the team began to try to regain control of the craft. John Credland, ESA head of science projects, said at the time, "Recovery will be a slow and careful operation. The main thing is that the spacecraft is now responding to us."

Return to life

Over the next three weeks the batteries slowly recharged. Eventually there was enough power to begin to thaw out some of SOHO's thrusters. Carefully using what little battery power they had, the team made delicate adjustments using the available thrusters. Over nine long days they stopped SOHO's spin and pointed it towards the Sun once more.

By the end of 1998 all of the instruments on board SOHO were working normally. Over ten years later SOHO is still helping scientists to understand how our star works.

SOHO sent back never before seen images of the Sun. The colours here are computer generated — the Sun doesn't look blue in space!

Other stars, other worlds

For centuries people have wondered about the existence of other worlds. In 1992, astronomers using a radio telescope discovered two rocky planets orbiting a neutron star. Since then, more than 490 **exoplanets** (a planet around another star) have been discovered.

Giant planets

The first discovery of a planet orbiting a star similar to the Sun came in 1995. It was somewhere between half and twice as big as Jupiter. So far all the discoveries have been of giant worlds like this.

Exoplanet Wasp 12B is so close to its star that it is being pulled apart by it.

Professor Sara Seager is a world expert on exoplanets. She works with the Kepler Space Telescope.

The hunt for other Earths

The search is on to find Earth-like worlds around other stars. A number of missions, using some of the most sensitive technology ever built, will join in the hunt. One of these is the Kepler Space Telescope, launched in 2009. Kepler is looking for planets using what is called the transit method. A transit occurs when a planet passes in front of its parent star. As it does so it blocks some of the light resulting in a slight dimming of the star. Kepler's sensitive instruments can detect this dimming if it takes place. Scientists can then use the measurements to calculate the size of the planet. Early indications in 2010 were that Kepler has indeed discovered many new worlds.

Spitzer surprises

In 2005, the Spitzer Space Telescope captured infrared light from two exoplanets. This marked the first time that light from worlds beyond the solar system had been observed. Two years later Spitzer detected evidence of water on an exoplanet and was able to produce the first exoplanet temperature map.

Flying in formation

One of NASA's aims for the future is to launch five spacecraft that will work together as if they were a single huge telescope. The spaceships will probably fly in formation, about a kilometre (less than a mile) apart. Four will have telescopes and the fifth will combine the results from the other four. The power of this multi-telescope should be sufficient to pick up the faint light of an Earth-like planet against the brighter light of its parent star.

The flecks of light in this stunning Hubble image are not stars — they are unimaginably distant galaxies, each containing billions of stars.

Telescopic time machines

The fastest thing in the Universe is light. It speeds across space from the stars to us at an astonishing 300,000 kilometres per second (186,000 miles per second). Even more astonishing is that even at that huge speed it still takes light four years to make the trip from the *nearest* star, Proxima Centauri.

Across the Universe

Using a telescope shows us things that are not only very far away in space, but also distant in time. Light from the most distant galaxies set out on its journey across space billions of years before Earth had even formed. Studying the light can help scientists understand how galaxies have changed over time.

Back to the beginning

Most scientists believe that the Universe came into existence in a Big Bang billions of years ago and it has been expanding ever since. Observations of deep space made by the Hubble Space Telescope and the WMAP Observatory have measured the faint radiation in space left over from the Big Bang. This has allowed scientists to estimate the age of the Universe. Currently the Universe is believed to be around 13.5 billion years old.

Furthest reaches

The Wide Field Camera 3 (WFC3) is the most advanced instrument aboard Hubble. It was installed during a space shuttle mission early in 2009. At the end of that year scientists obtained some remarkable images from the WFC3.

Shining faintly from the furthest reaches of the Universe are galaxies that are so far away that light left them 13 billion years ago, just a few hundred million years after the Universe is thought to have begun. Marcella Carollo was a member of the survey team that put together the data from WFC3. She described the distant galaxies as "the very building blocks from which the great galaxies of today, like our own **Milky Way**, ultimately formed". The scientists combined the Hubble data with data from the Spitzer Space Telescope to estimate the age and size of the galaxies.

"To our surprise, the results show that these galaxies... must have started forming stars hundreds of millions of years earlier, pushing back the time of the earliest star formation in the Universe."

Ivo Labbe, Spitzer Space Telescope team member

A dark Universe

Scientists have calculated that 96 per cent of the Universe is made up of dark matter and dark energy. This means that everything we see and know, including stars, planets, animals, and people, accounts for less than one-twentieth of the Universe.

These two galaxies are slowly colliding, pulled together by powerful gravitational forces. Over billions of years they will merge into one.

Where is everything?

One of the biggest mysteries for space scientists is trying to work out where most of the Universe actually is. Their calculations of how much material there is in the Universe don't make any sense. Unless, that is, most of the Universe is invisible to us.

How to weigh a galaxy

Obviously it isn't possible to weigh a galaxy the same way you might weigh potatoes. However, galaxies spin and it is possible to measure how fast they are rotating. The speed of the spin depends on the amount of mass (material) in the galaxy. Knowing one it is possible to work out the other.

The problem was that when scientists carried out their galaxy-weighing calculations, the results didn't come out the right way. The calculations indicated that there was five or six times more matter than we could actually see. What can this mysterious dark matter possibly be? We only know about it because of its gravity. It emits no light or any other form of energy.

Dark energy

As we saw earlier, the Universe is expanding. It isn't expanding steadily, however. The rate of expansion is getting faster. The reasons for this are mysterious. Perhaps we don't understand gravity as well as we thought. Or perhaps there is a strange form of "dark energy" at work. Dark matter, it seems, pulls the Universe together, while dark energy pulls it apart.

Chandra

One of the satellites currently being used to try to solve the problem is NASA's Chandra X-ray Observatory. By observing distant clusters of galaxies, Chandra has been able to see the effects of dark matter indirectly. Clouds of very hot gas lie between the galaxies in a cluster. The gases give off X-rays, which is how Chandra detects them. By observing how the gas clouds behave scientists can calculate where, and how massive, the dark matter is.

Being there

One of the volunteers for a simulated Mars mission prepares to spend 500 days in a mocked-up space capsule.

Most space scientists probably dream of actually being able to visit the stars and planets they study from afar. What does the future hold for human travel into deep space beyond the Moon?

The distant stars

The stars are so far away that we may never reach them. It is certainly unlikely that we would even attempt to at any time in the foreseeable future. Even Voyager 1, currently speeding from the solar system at over 60,000 kilometres per hour (37,282 miles per hour), would take around 75,000 years to cross the interstellar gulf to the nearest star.

Mission to Mars

Even a trip to the nearest planet, Mars, which some people think could take place around the 2030s, would mean a journey lasting more than a year for the crew. In May 2010, six volunteers were locked away in a mocked-up space module for over 500 days to simulate a flight to Mars.

How the volunteers react during the lengthy period they spend cooped up in the module will be of great help to mission planners for a real Mars mission. The mock spaceship also includes a Mars lander, and an area that has been made up to look like a Martian landscape. Three of the crew will also take part in a simulated Mars landing. Communication with the outside world will take place entirely by email to mimic the time delays there will be on an actual Mars voyage.

Humans versus robots

Perhaps the biggest difficulty to be faced in the human exploration of space is the humans themselves. Humans are big and heavy, they need food, water, and air to breathe, they need to be protected against radiation in space. Eventually they will also want to come home again! All this means having to build big powerful rockets to boost everything into space. At the moment, it is much more efficient to carry out our exploration of the Universe using telescopes and robot space probes that don't eat, sleep, or get bored on long journeys, and that can travel to places no human could survive.

One day, perhaps, human explorers really will visit the surface of Mars.

Is there anyone out there?

Is it possible that one day our probes will send back evidence that there are other living things in the Universe? Astrobiology is the study of the origin, evolution, and future of life in the Universe.

Three questions

NASA's Astrobiology Program looks for answers to three fundamental questions:

- How does life begin and evolve?
- Is there life beyond Earth?
- If there is, how can we detect it?

Experts in astronomy and astrophysics, Earth and planetary sciences, microbiology, evolutionary biology and **cosmochemistry** are all involved in this fascinating and cutting-edge branch of space exploration. Several space missions play a part in astrobiology research, such as the Spitzer and Kepler telescopes hunting for Earth-like planets, and the Mars rovers searching for traces of life on Mars.

Europa

Europa is one of Jupiter's larger moons (it is one of the four first seen by Galileo). Its surface is made of ice and scientists believe that there may be an ocean of liquid water underneath. Some astrobiologists think that there may be life in that ocean. Finding out will be tricky as it will involve not only a journey to Europa, but also having to drill as much as 100 kilometres (62 miles) through the ice. So far the deepest well drilled on Earth has been just 10.6 kilometres (6.5 miles) deep.

What secrets lie beneath the icy surface of Europa?

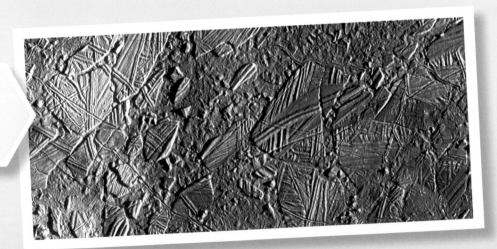

There is no reason to believe that Earth is the only place in the Universe where life has appeared. Just because we haven't detected it yet doesn't mean that it isn't there. It isn't possible to travel to the stars looking for life but we might still be able to find signs of it.

SETI

SETI is the Search for Extra-terrestrial Intelligence. Scientists are looking for life in other parts of the Universe by trying to find evidence of its technology. Radio telescopes are being used in an attempt to pinpoint evidence of transmissions from alien beings. So far, the search has proved fruitless. We have sent messages but no one has answered … at least not yet.

These are radio telescopes in the Allen Telescope Array in California, USA. They are part of SETI's mission to detect signals from alien civilizations.

WORD STATION
cosmochemistry branch of chemistry that deals with the chemistry of space

Timeline of space exploration

2296 BCE	Chinese astronomers make the first recorded observation of a comet.
763 BCE	Astronomers in Babylon (present-day Iraq) record seeing an eclipse of the Sun.
270 BCE	Aristarchus says the Sun is bigger than Earth and Earth goes around the Sun.
1609	Galileo Galilei builds one of the first telescopes and begins his groundbreaking discoveries.
1655	Christiaan Huygens improves the design of the telescope and discovers the rings of Saturn.
1687	Isaac Newton explains his ideas about gravity.
1781	William Herschel discovers that there are star systems beyond our galaxy.
1903	Russian scientist Konstantin Tsiolkovsky claims that space travel will be possible one day; later that year the Wright Brothers make the first powered flight.
1915	Proxima Centauri, the nearest star to Earth other than the Sun, is discovered.
1932	Karl Jansky tells the world about cosmic radio waves.
1957	The USSR launches the first satellite, Sputnik 1.
1957	Laika the dog becomes the first living creature to orbit Earth aboard Sputnik 2.
1959	The space probe Luna 3 sends back the first images of the far side of the Moon.
1961	Aboard his Vostok space capsule, Major Yuri Gagarin of the USSR becomes the first man to orbit Earth.
February 1966	Luna 9 makes the first controlled landing on the surface of the Moon.
1968	The crew of Apollo 8 are the first people from Earth to orbit the Moon.
1969	Apollo 11 astronauts Neil Armstrong and Edwin (Buzz) Aldrin are the first men to walk on the Moon.

1970	Venera 7 is the first probe to successfully land on the surface of Venus.
April 1971	Salyut 1, the first space station to orbit Earth, is launched.
November 1971	Mariner 9 reaches Mars and becomes the first space probe from Earth to orbit another planet.
1972	Apollo 17 returns to Earth from the Moon — there have been no more Moon missions to date.
1976	Viking 1 makes the first successful landing on Mars.
1980	Voyager 1 reaches Saturn and sends back the first detailed pictures of the ringed planet.
1989	Voyager 2 sends back the first close-up images of the planet Neptune.
25 April 1990	The Hubble Space Telescope is carried into orbit aboard the space shuttle Discovery.
1992	NASA launches SETI, the Search for Extra-terrestrial Intelligence.
1997	The remote-controlled Sojourner rover on Mars becomes the first human-made craft to travel over the surface of another planet.
2000	The first crew begins working aboard the International Space Station.
2005	The Huygens space probe lands on the surface of Titan, one of the moons of Saturn — it is the most distant landing ever made by an object from Earth.
January 2006	Samples from the Stardust mission to Comet Wild 2 reach Earth.
October 2006	The twin STEREO space probes are launched to study the Sun.
***2011**	MESSENGER is due to enter orbit around Mercury.
2011	Russia plans to launch Phobos-Grunt, a sample return mission to one of the moons of Mars.
2014	Rosetta is due to makes its rendezvous with a comet.
2015	New Horizon will make a fly-by of Pluto and the Kuiper belt.
2020	India and Japan plan manned landings on the Moon.

* Dates in 2011 and beyond are planned, but are subject to change.

Glossary

asteroid sometimes called minor planets, these are rocky objects orbiting the Sun in the solar system. Asteroids vary greatly in size.

astronomer person who studies objects and matter that are outside Earth's atmosphere

astronomy branch of science that studies everything beyond Earth's atmosphere, including planets, stars, and galaxies

atmosphere layer of gases or other objects in space that surround a planet

black hole region of space left by a star collapsing at the end of its life; a black hole's gravity is so powerful that not even light can escape it

comet fairly small (just a few kilometres across) icy object that orbits the Sun; when a comet approaches the Sun it produces a long tail of gas and dust

constellation pattern of stars in the night sky

cosmochemistry branch of chemistry that deals with the chemistry of space

electromagnetic spectrum range of radiation that travels through space in the form of waves; radio waves are the longest and X-rays and gamma rays are the shortest

exoplanet planet outside the solar system orbiting a star other than the Sun

galaxy collection of billions of stars

gravity force of attraction between all objects in the Universe; the more massive an object is the greater the force of gravity it exerts

gravity assist using the gravity of a planet to change the speed and flight path of a space probe

greenhouse gas gas in the atmosphere that absorbs heat and reflects it back to the surface rather than letting it escape into space

interstellar space space between the stars

Kuiper belt part of the solar system beyond the orbit of the planet Neptune; it is thought to be occupied by millions of comets and minor planets

meteorite space rock that crashes on to the surface of another larger object in space such as a moon or planet

Milky Way galaxy that contains the Sun and solar system

orbit move around an object in a circular manner, or the path on which an object moves around another object

sol word for a single day on Mars. A sol is 35 minutes, 39 seconds longer than a day on Earth.

solar panel device that converts light energy into electrical energy

solar system our Sun and its family of planets, asteroids, and other objects that orbit around it

space probe unmanned spaceship sent out to explore space

Universe everything that exists; all of space and everything in it

Find out more

Books

Backyard Guide to the Night Sky, Howard Schneider (National Geographic, 2009)

First Encyclopedia of Space, Paul Dowswell (Usborne Publishing, 2010)

Navigators: Star and Planets, Mike Goldsmith (Kingfisher, 2008)

Space, Paul Harrison (Franklin Watts, 2010)

Space Exploration, Steve Parker (Miles Kelly Publishing, 2009)

The Impact of Science and Technology: Space Exploration, Joseph Harris (Franklin Watts, 2009)

Websites

www.ukspaceagency.bis.gov.uk/Default.aspx
This is the website of the UK Space Agency. Learn what they do and find out more about space.

www.esa.int/esaCP/index.html
Learn more about space at the European Space Agency's website.

www.spacekids.co.uk/spacehistory/
This site includes a space timeline.

www.bbc.co.uk/science/space/
This site has information on the solar system, space exploration, life on Earth, and stars.

www.nasa.gov
The homepage of NASA, an excellent starting point for information on all aspects of space exploration.

http://hubblesite.org
The latest news and findings from the Hubble Space Telescope and links to a wealth of information on astronomy.

www.iwaswondering.org/heidi_homepage.html
Space scientist Heidi Hammel's child-friendly guide to space exploration.

Places to visit

National Space Centre
Exploration Drive
Leicester LE4 5NS
www.spacecentre.co.uk/Page.aspx/1/Home/

If you want to learn more about space, visit the National Space Centre. You can have a go at controlling a robot rover, see if you're sharp enough to be an astronaut, and create your own alien.

Science Museum
Exhibition Road
London SW7 2DD
www.sciencemuseum.org.uk/

Find out how the space age began and see rockets, space probes, and satellites.

Natural History Museum
Cromwell Road
London SW7 5BD
www.nhm.ac.uk/index.html

Visit the Natural History Museum to see their collection of meteorites.

Index

Akatsuki space probe 18–19
Apollo missions 14
Aristarchus (astronomer) 5
asteroids 15, 17, 20
astrobiology 40, 41
astronauts 14, 15, 38, 39
astronomers 5, 6–7, 10, 11, 24, 32, 40
atmospheres 7, 8, 9, 11, 19, 23, 28

Big Bang 35
brown dwarf stars 10
Burney, Venetia 26

carbon dioxide 19
Carollo, Marcella 35
Chandra X-ray Observatory 37
China 5, 15
comets 9, 24, 25
constellations 5
coronal mass ejections (CMEs) 29

dark energy 36, 37
Deep Space Network (DSN) 31
Discovery (space shuttle) 9
dwarf planets 26, 27

electromagnetic spectrum 10, 11
Europa (moon) 41
European Space Agency 19, 24, 30
exoplanets 32, 33

galaxies 10, 35, 36, 37
Galilei, Galileo 6–7, 41
gamma rays 11
Genesis space probe 28–29
gravity 23, 28, 36, 37
gravity assist 16, 17, 24
greenhouse gases 19
Grinspoon, David 19

Hammel, Heidi 9
Hazcams (hazard cameras) 21
Hubble Space Telescope 8, 9, 35

Imamura, Takeshi 19
India 5, 15

infrared waves 11, 19, 33
interstellar space 13, 38

James Webb Space Telescope 9
Japan 15, 18
Juno space probe 23
Jupiter 7, 9, 13, 22, 23, 41

Kepler Space Telescope 33, 40
Kuiper belt objects (KBOs) 24, 26, 27
Kuiper, Gerard 24

life 6, 14, 20, 28, 40, 41
light 7, 9, 10, 11, 13, 28, 31, 33, 35, 36
Lowell, Percival 6

Mariner space probes 6, 13, 16
Mars 6, 20, 21, 24, 39, 40
Mercury 16, 17, 19
Mercury Dual Imaging System (MDIS) 17
MESSENGER satellite 17
meteorites 15
Moon 5, 6, 10, 14–15, 20, 29
moons 7, 10, 12, 13, 20, 41

NASA 23, 30, 31, 33, 37, 40
Neptune 24
New Horizons space probe 26, 27
North Star 5

Opportunity rover 20, 21
Orton, Glenn 22

planetary scientists 12, 13, 22, 40
Pluto (dwarf planet) 26, 27
Prockter, Louise 17

radiation 11, 24, 35, 39
radio telescopes 10, 32, 41
radio waves 10, 21
Rosetta space probe 24, 25
rovers 20, 21, 40

satellites 11, 17, 18, 19, 29, 31, 37

Saturn 13, 20
Schiaparelli, Giovanni 6
SETI (Search for Extra-terrestrial Intelligence) 41
SOHO (Solar and Heliospheric Observatory) 30, 31
sols (Martian days) 20
Southern Equatorial Belt (SEB) 22, 23
space probes 6, 12, 13, 15, 16, 18–19, 20, 21, 23, 24, 25, 26, 27, 28–29, 30, 38, 39, 40
Spirit rover 20, 21
Spitzer Space Telescope 10, 11, 33, 35, 40
stars 5, 10, 11, 28, 30, 31, 32, 33, 35, 38, 41
STEREO (Solar Terrestrial Relations Observatory) 29
Stern, Alan 27
Student Dust Counter (SDC) 26
Sun 5, 6, 10, 11, 16, 19, 24, 28, 29, 30, 31
super-rotation 18–19

telescopes 6–7, 8, 9, 10, 11, 12, 14, 32, 33, 35, 39, 40, 41
temperatures 10, 11, 19, 33
Titan (moon) 20
transit method 33

Universe 6, 7, 9, 11, 35, 36, 37, 41

Venus 13, 16, 17, 18–19, 20
Venus Express space probe 19
Voyager 1 space probe 13, 38

weather 18, 29
Wide Field Camera 3 (WFC3) 35
winds 18–19, 22
WMAP Observatory 35

X-rays 11, 37